VOYAGE OF
THE LIBERDADE

Captain Joshua Slocum

DOVER PUBLICATIONS, INC.
Mineola, New York

Published in Canada by General Publishing Company, Ltd., 30 Lesmill Road, Don Mills, Toronto, Ontario.

Bibliographical Note

This Dover edition, first published in 1998, is an unabridged republication of the work first published by Robinson & Stephenson of Boston in 1890.

Library of Congress Cataloging-in-Publication Data

Slocum, Joshua, b. 1844.
    Voyage of the Liberdade / Joshua Slocum.
      p.   cm.
    "An unabridged republication of the work first published by Robinson & Stephenson of Boston in 1890"–T.p. verso.
    Includes bibliographical references (p.   –   ) and index.
    ISBN 0-486-40022-0 (pbk.)
    1. Slocum, Joshua, b. 1844–Journeys. 2. Liberdade (Ship) 3. Voyages and travels. I. Title.
G530.L61S56   1998
910.4'5–dc21   97-43864
                                                            CIP

Manufactured in the United States of America
Dover Publications, Inc., 31 East 2nd Street, Mineola, N.Y. 11501

CONTENTS

CHAPTER I: PAGE 1

The ship—The crew—A hurricane—Cape Verde Islands—Frio—A *pampeiro*.

CHAPTER II: PAGE 8

Montevideo—Beggars—Antonina for mate—Antonina to Buenos Aires—The *bombelia*.

CHAPTER III: PAGE 11

Salvage of a cargo of wine—Sailors happy—Cholera in the Argentine —Death in the land—Dutch Harry—Pete the Greek—Noted crimps— Boat lost—Sail for Ilha Grande—Expelled from the port—Serious hardships.

CHAPTER IV: PAGE 20

Ilha Grande decree—Return to Rosario—Waiting opening of the Brazilian ports—Scarcity of sailors—Buccaneers turned pilots—Sail down the river—Arrive at Ilha Grande the second time—Quarantined and fumigated—Admitted to *pratique*—Sail for Rio—Again challenged —Rio at last.

CHAPTER V: PAGE 27

At Rio—Sail for Antonina with mixed cargo—A *pampeiro*—Ship on beam-ends—Cargo still more mixed—Topgallant-masts carried away— Arrive safely at Antonina.

CONTENTS

CHAPTER VI: PAGE 30

Mutiny—Attempt at robbery and murder—Four against one—Two go down before a rifle—Order restored.

CHAPTER VII: PAGE 37

Join the bark at Montevideo—A good crew—Small-pox breaks out— Bear up for Maldonado and Flores—No aid—Death of sailors—To Montevideo in distress—Quarantine.

CHAPTER VIII: PAGE 46

A new crew—Sail for Antonina—Load timber—Native canoes—Loss of the *Aquidneck*.

CHAPTER IX: PAGE 51

The building of the *Liberdade*.

CHAPTER X: PAGE 63

Across the bar—The run to Santos—Tow to Rio by the steamship— At Rio.

CHAPTER XI: PAGE 70

Sail from Rio—Anchor at Cape Frio—Encounter with a whale— Sunken treasure—The schoolmaster—The merchant—The good people at the village—A pleasant visit.

CONTENTS

CHAPTER XII: PAGE 76

Sail from Frio—Round Cape St. Thome—High seas and swift currents —In the "trades"—Dangerous reefs—Run into harbour unawares, on a dark and stormy night—At Caravellas—Fine weather—A gale— Port St. Paulo—Treacherous natives—Sail for Bahia.

CHAPTER XIII: PAGE 81

At Bahia—Meditations on the discoverers—The Caribbees.

CHAPTER XIV: PAGE 84

Bahia to Pernambuco—The meeting of the *Finance* at sea—At Pernambuco—Round Cape St. 'Roque—A gale—Breakers—The stretch to Barbadoes—Flying-fish alighting on deck—Dismasted—Arrive at Carlysle Bay.

CHAPTER XV: PAGE 95

At Barbadoes—Mayaguez—Crossing the Bahama Banks—The Gulf Stream—Arrival on the coast of South Carolina.

CHAPTER XVI: PAGE 107

Ocean Currents—Visit to South Santee—At the Typee River—Quarantined—South Port and Wilmington, N.C.—Inland sailing to Beaufort, Norfolk and Washington, D.C.—Voyage ended.

DISPOSAL OF THE LIBERDADE: PAGE 117

vii

CONTENTS

LIST OF ILLUSTRATIONS

Diagram of the *Liberdade* 52

The *Liberdade* 62

MAP

Course of the *Liberdade* from Paranagua to Barbadoes 69

GREETING

THIS literary craft of mine, in its native model and rig, goes out laden with the facts of the strange happenings on a home afloat. Her constructor, a sailor for many years, could have put a whole cargo of salt, so to speak, in the little packet; but would not so wantonly intrude on this domain of longshore navigators. Could the author and constructor but box-haul, club-haul, tops'l-haul, and catharpin like the briny sailors of the strand, ah me!—and hope to be forgiven!

Be the current against us, what matters it? Be it in our favour, we are carried hence, to what place or for what purpose? Our plan of the whole voyage is so insignificant that it matters little, maybe, whither we go, for the "grace of a day" is the same! Is it not a recognition of this which makes the old sailor happy, though in the storm; and hopeful even on a plank in mid-ocean? Surely it is this! for the spiritual beauty of the sea, absorbing man's soul, permits of no infidels on its boundless expanse.

THE AUTHOR.

viii

CHAPTER I

The ship—The crew—A hurricane—Cape Verde Islands—Frio—
A *pampeiro*.

To get underweigh: It was on the 28th of February
1886, that the bark *Aquidneck*, laden with case-oil'
sailed from New York for Montevideo, the capital o'
Uruguay, the strip of land bounding the River Plate
on the east, and called by the natives "Banda Oriental."
The *Aquidneck* was a trim and tidy craft of 326 tons'
register, hailing from Baltimore, the port noted for
clippers, and being herself high famed above them all
for swift sailing, she had won admiration on many
seas.

Her crew mustered ten, all told; twelve had been
the complement, when freights were good. There were,
beside the crew with regular stations, a little lad, aged
about six years, and his mamma (age immaterial),
privileged above the rest, having "all nights in"—that
is, not having to stand watch. The mate, Victor, who is
to see many adventures before reaching New York
again, was born and bred on shipboard. He was in
perfect health, and as strong as a windlass. When he
first saw the light and began to give orders, he was at
San Francisco on the packet *Constitution*, the vessel lost
in the tempest at Samoa, just before the great naval
disaster at the same place in the year of 1889. Garfield,
the little lad above mentioned, Victor's brother, in this
family ship, was born in Hong Kong harbour, in the old
bark *Amethyst*, a bona-fide American citizen, though first
seeing the light in a foreign port, the Stars and Stripes
standing sponsors for his nationality. This bark had

1

braved the wind and waves for fifty-eight years, but had not, up to that date, so far as I know, experienced so lively a breeze as the one which sprung up about her old timbers on that eventful 3rd of March, 1880.

Our foremast hands on the *Aquidneck*, six in number, were from as many nations, strangers to me and strangers to each other; but the cook, a negro, was a native American—to the manner born. To have even so many Americans in one ship was considered exceptional.

Much or little as matters this family history and description of the crew: the day of our sailing was bitter-cold and stormy, boding no good for the coming voyage, which was to be, indeed, the most eventful of my life of more than five-and-thirty years at sea. Studying the morning weather report, before sailing, we saw predicted a gale from the nor'west, and one also approaching from the sou'west at the same time. "The prospect," said the New York papers, "is not encouraging." We were anxious, however, to commence the voyage, having a crew on board, and, being all ready, we boldly sailed, somewhat against our better judgment. The nor'-wester blowing, at the time, at the rate of forty miles an hour, increased to eighty or ninety miles by March 2nd. This hurricane continued through March 3rd, and gave us serious concern for the ship and all on board.

At New York, on those days, the wind howled from the north, with the "storm centre somewhere on the Atlantic," so said the wise seamen of the weather bureau, to whom, by the way, the real old salt is indebted, at the present day, for information of approaching storms, sometimes days ahead. The prognostication was correct, as we can testify, for out on the Atlantic our bark could carry only a mere rag of a foresail, somewhat larger than a table-cloth, and with this storm-sail she went flying before the tempest, all those dark days, with a large "bone in her mouth,"[1] making great headway, even under the small sail. Mountains of seas swept clean over the bark in their mad race, filling her decks full to the top of the bulwarks, and shaking things generally.

Our men were lashed, each one to his station; and all spare spars not doubly lashed were washed away, along with other movables that were broken and torn from their fastenings by the wild storm.

The cook's galley came in for its share of the damage, the cook himself barely escaping serious injury from a sea that went thundering across the decks, taking with it doors, windows, galley stove, pots, kettles and all, together with the culinary artist; landing the whole wreck in the lee scuppers, but, most fortunately, with the professor on top. A misfortune like this is always—felt. It dampens one's feelings, so to speak. It means cold food for a time to come, if not even worse fare.

The day following our misfortune, however, was not so bad. In fact, the tremendous seas boarding the bark latterly were indications of the good change coming, for it meant that her speed had slackened through a lull of the gale, allowing the seas to reach her too full and heavy.

More sail was at once crowded on, and still more was set at every stage of the abatement of the gale, for the craft should not be lazy when big seas race after her. And so on we flew, like a scud, sheeting home sail after sail as required, till the 5th of March, when all of her white wings were spread, and she fairly "walked the waters like a thing of life." There was now wind enough

[1] The white foam at the bows produced by fast sailing is, by sailors, called "a bone in her mouth."

for several days, but not too much, and our swift-sailing craft laughed at the seas trying to catch her.

Cheerily on we sailed for days and days, pressed by the favouring gale, meeting the sun each day a long span earlier, making daily four degrees of longitude. It was the time, on these bright days, to forearm with dry clothing against future stormy weather. Boxes and bags were brought on deck, and drying and patching went on by wholesale in the watch below, while the watch on deck bestirred themselves putting the ship in order. "Chips," the carpenter, mended the galley; the cook's broken shins were plastered up; and in a few days all was well again . And the sailors, moving cheerfully about once more in their patched garments of varied hues, reminded me of the spotted cape pigeons pecking for a living, the pigeons, I imagined, having a better life of the two. A panican of hot coffee or tea by sailors called "water bewitched," a sea-biscuit, and "bit of salt-horse," had regaled the crew and restored their voices. Then "Reuben Ranzo" was heard on the breeze, and the main tack was boarded to the tune of "Johnny Boker." Other wondrous songs through the night-watch could be heard in keeping with the happy time. Then what they would do and what they wouldn't do in the next port was talked of, when song and yarn ran out.

Hold fast, shipmate, hold fast and belay! or the crimps of Montevideo will wear the new jacket you promise yourself, while you will be off Cape Horn, singing "Haul out to leeward," with a wet stocking on your neck, and with the same old "lamby" on, that long since was "lamby" only in name, the woolly part having given way to a cloth worn much in "Far Cathay"; in short, you will dress in dungaree, the same as now, while the crimps and landsharks divide your

4

scanty earnings, unless you "take in the slack" of your feelings, and "make all fast and steady all."

Ten days out, and we were in the northeast "trades" —porpoises were playing under the bows as only porpoises can play; dolphins were racing alongside, and flying-fish were all about. This was, indeed, a happy change, and like being transported to another world. Our hardships were now all forgotten, for "the sea washes off all the woes of men."

One week more of pleasant sailing, all going orderly on board, and Cape Verde Islands came in sight. A grand and glorious sight they were! All hail, *terra firma*! It is good to look at you once again! By noon the islands were abeam, and the fresh trade-wind in the evening bore us out of sight of them before dark.

Most delightful sailing is this large, swinging motion of our bark bounding over the waves, with the gale abaft the beam, driving her forward till she fairly leaps from billow to billow, as if trying to rival her companions, the very flying-fish. Thwarted now by a sea, she strikes it with her handsome bows, sending into the light countless thousand sprays, that shine like a nimbus of glory. The tread on her deck-plank is lighter now, and the little world afloat is gladsome fore and aft.

Cape Frio (cold cape) was the next landfall. Upon reaching that point, we had crossed the Atlantic twice. The course toward Cape Verde Islands had been taken to avail ourselves of a leading wind through the southeast trades, the course from the islands to Frio being southwesterly. This latter stretch was spanned on an easy bow-line; with nothing eventful to record. Thence our course was through variable winds to the River Plate, where a *pampeiro* was experienced that blew "great guns," and whistled a hornpipe through the rigging.

These *pampeiros* (winds from the *pampas*) usually blow with great fury, but give ample warning of their approach: the first sign being a spell of unsurpassed fine weather, with small, fleecy clouds floating so gently in the sky that one scarcely perceives their movements, yet they do move, like an immense herd of sheep grazing undisturbed on the great azure field. All this we witnessed, and took into account. Then gradually, and without any apparent cause, the clouds began to huddle together in large groups; a sign had been given which the elements recognized. Next came a flash of fire from behind the accumulating masses, then a distant rumbling noise. It was a note of warning, and one that no vessel should let pass unheeded. "Clew up, and furl!" was the order. To hand all sail when these fierce visitors are out on a frolic over the seas, and entertain them under bare poles, is the safest plan, unless, indeed, the best storm sails are bent; even then it is safest to goose-wing the tops'ls before the gale comes on. Not till the fury of the blast is spent does the ship require sail, for it is not till then that the sea begins to rise, necessitating sail to steady her.

The first onslaught of the storm, levelling all before it, and sending the would-be waves flying across in sheets—sailor sheets, so to speak—lends a wild and fearful aspect; but there is no dread of a lee-shore in the sailor's heart at these times, for the gale is from off the land, as indicated by the name it bears.

After the gale was a calm; following which came desirable winds, that carried us at last to the port we sought—Montevideo; where we cast anchor on the 5th of May, and made preparations, after the customs' visit, for discharging the cargo, which was finally taken into lighters from alongside to the piers, and thence to the warehouses, where ends the ship's responsibility to the owner of the goods. But not till then ceases the ship's liability, or the captain's care of the merchandise placed in his trust. Clearly the captain has cares on sea and on land.

CHAPTER II

Montevideo—Beggars—Antonina for maté—Antonina to Bueno, Aires—The *bombelia*.

MONTEVIDEO, sister city to Buenos Aires, is the fairer of the two to look upon from the sea, having a loftier situation, and, like Buenos Aires, boasts of many fine mansions, comely women, liberal schools, and a cemetery of great splendour.

It is at Montevideo that the "beggar a-horse-back" becomes a verity (horses are cheap); galloping up to you the whining beggar will implore you, saying: "For the love of Christ, friend, give me a coin to buy bread with."

From "the Mont" we went to Antonina, in Brazil, for a cargo of maté, a sort of tea, which, prepared as a drink, is wholesome and refreshing. It is partaken of by the natives in a highly sociable manner, through a tube which is thrust into the steaming beverage in a silver urn or a calabash, whichever may happen to be at hand when "drouthy neebors neebors meet"; then all sip and sip in bliss from the same tube, which is passed from mouth to mouth. No matter how many mouths there may be, the *bombelia*, as it is called, must reach them all. It may have to be replenished to make the drink go around, and several times, too, when the company is large. This is done with but little loss of time. By thrusting into the urn or gourd a spoonful of the herb, and two spoonfuls of sugar to a pint of water, which is poured, boiling, over it, the drink is made. But to give it some fancied extra flavour, a live coal (*carbo vegetable*) is plunged into the potion to the bottom.

Then it is again passed around, beginning where it left off. Happy is he, if a stranger, who gets the first sip at the tube, but the initiated have no prejudices. While in that country I frequently joined in the social rounds at maté, and finally rejoiced in a *bombelia* of my own.

The people at Antonina (in fact all the people we saw in Brazil) were kind, extremely hospitable, and polite; living in thrift generally, their wants were but few beyond their resources. The mountain scenery, viewed from the harbour of Antonina, is something to gloat over; I have seen no place in the world more truly grand and pleasing. The climate, too, is perfect and healthy. The only doctor of the place, when we were there, wore a coat out at the elbows, for lack of patronage. A desirable port is Antonina.

We had musical entertainments on board, at this place. To see the display of beautiful white teeth by these Brazilian sweet singers was good to the soul of a sea-tossed mariner. One nymph sang for the writer's benefit a song at which they all laughed very much. Being in native dialect, I did not understand it, but of course laughed with the rest, at which they were convulsed; from this, I supposed it to be at my expense. I enjoyed that, too, as much, or more, than I would have relished *areytos* in my favour.

With maté we came to Buenos Aires, where the process of discharging the cargo was the same as at Montevideo—into lighters. But at Buenos Aires, we lay four times the distance from the shore, about four miles.

The herb, or *herva maté*, is packed into barrels, boxes, and into bullock-hide sacks, which are sewed up with stout hide thongs. The contents, pressed in tightly when the hide is green and elastic, becomes as hard as a cannon-ball by the contraction which follows when it dries. The first load of the *soroes*, so-called, that came off to the bark at the port of loading, was espied on the way by little Garfield. Piled in the boat, high above the gunwales, the hairy side out, they did look odd. "Oh, papa," said he, "here comes a load of cows! Stand by, all hands, and take them in."

CHAPTER III

Salvage of a cargo of wine—Sailors happy—Cholera in the Argentine—Death in the land—Dutch Harry—Pete the Greek —Noted crimps—Boat lost—Sail for Ilha Grande—Expelled from the port—Serious hardships.

FROM Buenos Aires, we proceeded up the River Plate, near the confluence of the Parana and Paraguay, to salve a cargo of wine from the stranded brig *Neovo San Pascual*, from Marseilles.

The current of the great river at that point runs constantly seaward, becoming almost a sea of itself, and a dangerous one to navigate; hence the loss of the *San Pascual*, and many others before her.

If, like the "Ancient Mariner," we had, any of us, cried, "water, water all around, and not a drop to drink," we forgot it now, in this bountiful stream. Wine, too, we had without stint. The insurance agent, to leave no excuse for tampering with the cargo, rolled out a cask of the best, and, like a true Hans Breitmann, "knocked out der bung." Then, too, cases were broken in the handling, the contents of which drenched their clothes from top to toe, as the sailors carried them away on their heads.

The diversity of a sailor's life—ah me! The experience of Dana and his shipmates, for instance, on a sunburnt coast, carrying dry hides on their heads, if not a worse one, may be in store for us, we cried, now fairly swimming in luxuries—water and wine alike free. Although our present good luck may be followed by times less cheerful, we preferred to count this, we said, as compensation for past misfortunes, marking well that "it never rains but it pours."

11

The cargo of wine in due course was landed at Rosario with but small loss, the crew, except in one case, remaining sober enough to help navigate even the difficult Parana. But one old sinner, the case I speak of, an old Labrador fisherman, became a useless, drunken swab, in spite of all we could do. I say "we" for most of the crew were on my side, in favour of a fair deal and "regular supplies."

The hold was barred and locked, and every place we could think of, for a time, was searched; still Dan kept terribly drunk. At last his mattress was turned out, and from it rolled a dozen or more bottles of the best liquor. Then there was a row, but all on the part of Dan, who swore blue vengeance on the man, if he could but find him out, who had stowed that grog in his bunk, "trying to get" him "into trouble"; some of those "young fellows would rue it yet!"

The cargo of wine being discharged, I chartered to load alfalfa, packed in bales, for Rio. Many deaths had occurred about this time, with appalling suddenness; we soon learned that cholera was staring us all in the face, and that it was fast spreading through the country, filling towns and cities with sickness and death.

Approaching more frightfully near, it carried our pilot over the bar; his wife was a widow the day after he brought our bark to the loading berth. And the young man who commenced to deliver us the cargo was himself measured the day after. His ship had come in!

Many stout men, and many, many women and children succumbed to the scourge; yet it was our high privilege to come through the dark cloud without losing a loved one, while thousands were cast down with bereavements and grief. At one time it appeared that we were in the centre of the cloud which zig-zagged its ugly body, serpent-like, through districts, poisoning all that it touched, and leaving death in its wake. This was indeed cholera in its most terrible form!

One poor fellow sat at the Widow Lacinas' hotel, bewildered. "Forty-eight hours ago," said he, "I sat at my own hearth, with wife and three children by my side. Now I am alone in the world! Even my poor house, such as it was, is pulled down." This man, I say, had troubles; surely was his "house pulled down!"

There was no escaping the poison or keeping it off, except by disinfectants, and by keeping the system regular, for it soon spread over all the land and the air was full of it. Remedies sold so high that many must have perished without the test of medicinal aid to cure their disease. A cry went up against unprincipled druggists who were over-charging for their drugs, but nothing more was done to check their greed. Camphor sold as high as four dollars a pound, and the druggist with a few hundred drops of laudanum and as much chlorodyne could travel through Europe afterward on the profits of his sales.

It was at Rosario, and at this time, that we buried our young friend, Captain Speck, well loved of young and old. His friends did not ask whether it was cholera or not that he died of, but performed the last act of friendship as became men of heart and feeling. The minister could not come that day, but Captain Speck's little friend, Garfield, said: "The flags were set for the angels to come and take the Captain to Heaven!" Need more be said?

And the flags blew out all day.

Then it became us to erect a memorial slab, and, hardest of all, to write to the widow and orphans. This was done in a homely way, but with sympathetic, aching hearts away off there in Santa Fè.

Our time at Rosario, after this, was spent in gloomy

days that dragged into weeks and months, and our thoughts often wandered from there to a happy past. We preferred to dwell away from there and in other climes, if only in thought. There was, however, one happy soul among us—the child whose face was a sunbeam in all kinds of weather and at all times, happy in his ignorance of the evils that fall to the lot of man.

Our sailing-day from Rosario finally came; and, with a feeling as of casting off fetters, the lines were let go, and the bark hauled out into the stream, with a full cargo on board; but, instead of sailing for Rio, as per charter, she was ordered by the Brazilian consul to Ilha Grande (Great Island), the quarantine station of Brazil, some sixty-two miles west of Rio, there to be disinfected and to discharge her cargo in quarantine.

A new crew was shipped and put aboard, but while I was getting my papers, about noon, they stole one of the ship's boats and scurried off down the river as fast, no doubt, as they could go. I have not seen them or my boat since. They all deserted,—every mother's son of them! taking, beside the boat, a month's advance pay from a Mr. Dutch Harry, a sailor boarding-master, who had stolen my inward crew that he might, as he boasted afterward, "ship new hands in their places." In view of the fact that this vilest of crimps was the loser of the money, I could almost forgive the "galoots" for the theft of my boat. (The ship is usually responsible for advance wages twenty-four hours after she has sailed, providing, too, that the sailors proceed to sea in her.) Seeing, moreover, that they were of that stripe, unworthy the name of sailor, my vessel was the better without them, by at least what it cost to be rid of them, namely, the price of my boat.

However, I will take back what I said about Dutch Harry being the "vilest crimp." There came one to

Rosario worse than he, one "Pete the Greek," who cut off the ears of a rival boarding-master at the Boca, threw them into the river, then, making his escape to Rosario, some 180 miles away, established himself in the business in opposition to the Dutchman, whom he "shanghaied" soon after, then "reigned peacefully in his stead."

A captain who, like myself, had suffered from the depredations of this noted gentry, told me, in great glee, that he saw Harry on a bone-laden Italian bark outward bound,—"even then nearly out of the river." The last seen of him by my friend, the captain, was "among the branches," with a rope around his neck— they hanged him, maybe—I don't know what else the rope was for, or who deserved more to be hanged. The captain screamed with delight:—"he'll get bone soup, at least, for a while, instead of Santa Fè good mutton-chops at our expense."

My second crew was furnished by Mr. Pete, before referred to, and on the seventeenth of December we set sail from that country of revolutions. Things soon dropped into working order, and I found reason to be pleased with the change of crew We glided smoothly along down the river, thence wishing never again to see Rosario under the distressing circumstances through which she had just passed.

On the following day, while slipping along before a light, rippling breeze, a dog was espied out in the current, struggling in the whirlpools, which were rather strong, apparently unable to extricate himself, and was greatly exhausted. Coming up with him our main-tops'l was laid to the mast, and as we ranged by the poor thing, a sailor, plunging over the side in a bow-line, bent a rope on to doggy, another one hauled him carefully on board, and the rescue was made. He proved to be a fine young retriever, and his intelligent signs of thankfulness for his escape from drowning were scarcely less eloquent of gratitude than human spoken language.

This pleasant incident happening on a Friday, suggested, of course, the name we should give him. His new master, to be sure, was Garfield, who at once said, "I guess they won't know me when I get home, with my new suit—and a dog!" The two romped the decks thenceforth, early and late. It was good to see them romp, while "Friday" "barkit wi' joy."

Our pets were becoming numerous now, and all seemed happy till a stowaway cat one day killed poor little "Pete," our canary. For ten years or more we had listened to the notes of this wee bird, in many countries and climes. Sweetest of sweet singers, it was buried in the great Atlantic at last. A strange cat, a careless steward, and its tiny life was ended—and the tragedy told. This was indeed a great loss to us all, and was mourned over,—almost as the loss of a child.

A book that has been read at sea has a near claim on our friendship, and is a thing one is loth to part with, or change, even for a better book. But the well-tried friend of many voyages is oh! so hard to part with at sea. A resting-place in the solemn sea of sameness—in the trackless ocean, marked only by imaginary lines and circles—is a cheerless spot to look to; yet how many have treasures there!

Returning to the voyage and journal: Our pilot proved incompetent, and we narrowly escaped shipwreck in consequence at Martin Garcia Bar, a bad spot in the River Plate. A small schooner captain, observing that we needlessly followed in his track, and being anything but a sailor in principle, wantonly meditated mischief to us. While I was confidently trusting to my pilot, and he (the pilot) trusting to the schooner, one that could go over banks where we would strike, what did the scamp do but shave close to a dangerous spot, my pilot following faithfully in his wake. Then, jumping upon the taffrail of his craft, as we came abreast the shoal, he yelled, like a Comanche, to my pilot to: "Port the helm!" and what does my mutton-headed jackass do but port hard over! The bark, of course, brought up immediately on the ground, as the other had planned, seeing which his whole pirate crew—they could have been little less than pirates—joined in roars of laughter, but sailed on, doing us no other harm.

By our utmost exertions the bark was gotten off, not a moment too soon, however, for by the time we kedged her into deep water a *pampeiro* was upon us. She rode out the gale safe at anchor, thanks to an active crew. Our water tanks and casks were then refilled, having been emptied to lighten the bark from her perilous position.

Next evening the storm went down, and by mutual consent our mud-pilot left, taking passage in a passing river-craft, with his pay and our best advice, which was to ship in a dredging-machine, where his capabilities would be appreciated.

Then, "paddling our own canoe," without further accident we reached the light-ship, passing it on Christmas Day. Clearing thence, before night, English Bank and all other dangers of the land, we set our course for Ilha Grande, the wind being fair. Then a sigh of relief was breathed by all on board. If ever "old briny" was welcomed, it was on that Christmas Day.

Nothing further of interest occurred on the voyage to Brazil, except the death of the little bird already spoken of, which loss deeply affected us all.

We arrived at Ilha Grande, our destination, on the 7th day of January, 1887, and came to anchor in nine fathoms of water, at about noon, within musket-range of the guard-ship, and within speaking distance of several vessels riding quarantine, with more or less communication going on among them all, through flags. Several ships, chafing under the restraint of quarantine, were "firing signals" at the guard-ship. One Scandinavian, I remember, asked if he might be permitted to communicate by *cable* with his owners in Christiana. The guard gave him, as the Irishman said, "an evasive answer," so the cablegram, I suppose, laid over. Another wanted police assistance; a third wished to know if he could get fresh provisions—ten milreis' ($5) worth (he was a German)—naming a dozen or more articles that he wished for, "and *the balance in onions!*" Altogether, the young fellows on the guard-ship were having, one might say, a signal practice.

On the next day, January 8th, the officers of the port came alongside in a steam-launch, and ordered us to leave, saying the port had been closed that morning. "But we have made the voyage," I said. "No matter," said the guard, "leave at once you must, or the guard-ship will fire into you." This, I submit, was harsh and arbitrary treatment. A thunderbolt from a clear sky could not have surprised us more or worked us much greater harm—to be ruined in business or struck by lightning, being equally bad!

Then pointing something like a gun, Dom Pedro said, said he, "*Vaya Homem*" (hence, begone), "Or you'll give us cholera." So back we had to go, all the way to Rosario, with that load of hay—and trouble. But on our arrival there we found things better than they were when we sailed. The cholera had ceased—it was on the wane when we sailed from Rosario, and there was hardly a case of the dread disease in the whole country east of Cordova when we returned. That was, indeed, a comfort, but it left our hardship the same, and led, consequently, to the total loss of the vessel after dragging us through harrowing trials and losses, as will be seen by subsequent events.

CHAPTER IV

Ilha Grande decree—Return to Rosario—Waiting opening of the
Brazilian ports—Scarcity of sailors—Buccaneers turned pilots
—Sail down the river—Arrive at Ilha Grande the second
time—Quarantined and fumigated—Admitted to *pratique*—
Sail for Rio—Again challenged—Rio at last.

THIS Ilha Grande decree, really a political movement, brought great hardships on us, notwithstanding that it was merely intended by the Brazilians as
retaliation for past offences by their Argentine neigh-
bours; not only for quarantines against Rio fevers, but
for a discriminating duty as well on sugar from the
empire; a combination of hardships on commerce—
more than the sensitive Brazilians could stand—so
chafing them that a retaliation fever sprung up reaching more than the heat of *febre marello,* and they decided
to teach their republican cousins a wholesome lesson.
However, their wish was to retaliate without causing
war, and it was done. In fact, closing ports as they did
at the beginning of Argentine's most valuable season of
exports to Brazil, and with the plausible excuse, namely
fear of pain in the stomach, so filled the Argentines
with admiration of their equals in strategy that they
on the earliest opportunity proclaimed two public holi-
days in honour of bright Brazil. So the matter of dif-
ference ended, to the delight of all—in fire-crackers and
champagne!

To the delight of all except the owner and crew of
the *Aquidneck.* For our bark there was no way but to
return where the cargo came from, at a ruinous loss,
too, of time and money. We called at the first open port

and wired to the owner of the cargo, but got no answer. Thence we sailed to Buenos Aires, where I telegraphed again for instructions. The officers of the guard-ship, upon receiving my report from Brazil, were convulsed with laughter, while I—— I confess it—could not see the joke. After waiting two days, this diplomatic reply came from the owner of the cargo: "Act as the case may require." Upon this matter I had several opinions. One person suggested that the case required me to pitch the whole cargo into the sea! This friend, I may mention, was from Boston.

I have ever since regretted, however, that I did not take his advice. There seemed to be no protection for the vessel; the law that a ship must be allowed to live was unheeded; in fact this law was reversed and there were sharpers and beach-combers at every turn ready to take advantage of one's misfortunes or even drive one to despair. I concluded, finally, to shake the lot of them, and proceeding up the Parana, moored again at the berth where, a few weeks before, we had taken in the cargo. Spans and tackle were rigged, and all was made read to discharge. It was now, "Come on, McCarthy, or McCarthy, come on!" I didn't care which, I had one *right* on my side, and I kept that always in view; namely, the right to discharge the cargo where I had first received it; but where the money to buy ballast and pay other charges was to come from I could not discover.

My merchant met me in great concern at my "misfortunes," but "carramba!" (zounds) said he, "my own losses are great." It required very little reasoning to show me that the least expensive course was the safest one for me to adopt, and my merchant offering enough to pay the marketing, I found it wisest not to disturb the cargo, but to lay up instead with it in the vessel and await the reopening of the Brazilian ports. This I did.

My merchant, Don Manuel, is said to be worth millions of *pesos*. The foundation of his wealth was laid by peddling charcoal, carrying it at first, to his credit be it said, on his back, and he was then a good fellow. Many a hard bargain has he waged since, and is now a "Don," living in a $90,000 house. The Don doesn't peddle charcoal any more.

Moored at Rosario, waiting, waiting; but all of us well in body, and myself finally less agitated in mind. My old friend, Don Manuel, seems better also; he "may yet purge and live clean like a gentleman."

I found upon our return to Rosario that some of the old hands were missing; laid low by the scourge, to make room for others, and some were spared who would have been less lamented. Among all the ship-brokers that I knew at Rosario, and I knew a great many, not one was taken away. They all escaped, being, it was thought, epidemic-proof. There was my broker, Don Christo Christiano—called by Don Manuel "El Sweaga" (the Swede)—whom nothing could strike with penetrative force, except a commission.

At last, April 9th, 1887, news came that the Brazilian ports were open. Cholera had long since disappeared in Santa Fè and Buenos Aires. The Brazilians had established their own beef-drying factories, and could now afford to open their ports to competition. This made a great stir among the ships. Crews were picked up here and there, out of the few brothels that had not been pulled down during the cholera, and out of the streets or from the fields. Some, too, came in from the bush. Mixed among them were many that had been let out of the prisons all over the country, so that the scourge should not be increased by over-crowded jails. Of six who shipped with me, four had been so released from prison, where they had been serving for murder or highway robbery; all this I learned when it was too late. I shall have occasion before long to speak of these again!

Well, we unmoored and dropped down the river a few miles the first day; with this crew, the hardest looking set that ever put foot on a ship of mine, and with a swarthy Greek pilot that would be taken for a pirate in any part of the world. The second mate, who shipped also at Rosario, was not less ill-visaged, and had, in addition to his natural ugly features, a deep scar across his face, suggestive of a heavy sabre stroke; a mark which, I thought upon further acquaintance, he had probably merited. I could not make myself easy upon the first acquaintance of my new and decidedly ill-featured crew. So, early the first evening I brought the bark to anchor, and made all snug before dark for prudent reasons. Next morning, the Greek, instead of getting the bark underweigh, as I expected him to do, came to me demanding more pay for his services and thinking, maybe, that I could not do without him, demanded, unless I chose to pay considerably in excess of his regular dues, to be put on shore. I took the fellow at his first bounce. He and his grip-sack were landed on the bank there and then, with but little "palaver" over it. It was then said, so I learned after, that "old S——" would drop into the wake of some ship, and save his pilotage; in fact, they didn't know "what else he could do," as the pilots were then all engaged for other vessels.

The money was taken care of all right, and so was the *Aquidneck*! By daylight of the following morning she was underweigh, and under full sail at the head of a fleet of piloted vessels, and, being the swiftest sailer, easily kept the lead, and was one of the vessels that did *not* "*rompe el banco*," as was predicted by all the pilots, while

23

they hunched their shoulders above their ears, exclaiming, "No *practico*, no *possebla!*" This was my second trip down the Parana, it is true, and I had been on other rivers as wonderful as this one, and had, moreover, read Mark Twain's "Life on the Mississippi," which gives no end of information on river currents, wind-reefs, sand-reefs, alligator-water, and all that is useful to know about rivers, so that I was confident of my ability; all that had been required was the stirring-up that I got from the impertinent pilot, or buccaneer, whichever is proper to call him—one thing certain, he was no true sailor!

A strong, fair wind on the river, together with the current, in our favour, carried us flying down the channel, while we kept the lead, with the Stars and Stripes waving where they ought always to be seen; namely, on the ship in the van! So the duffers followed us, instead of our following them, and on we came, all clear, with the good wishes of the officers and the crews. But the pilots, drawing their shoulders up and repeating the refrain, "No *practico*, no *possebla!*" cursed us bitterly, and were in a vile mood, I was told, cursing more than usual, and that is saying a great deal, for all will agree who have heard them that the average "Dago" pilot is the most foul-mouthed thing afloat.

Down the river and past the light-ship we came once more, this time with no halt to make, no backing sails to let a pilot off, nothing at all to stop us; we spread all sail to a favourable breeze, and reached Ilha Grande eight days afterward, beating the whole fleet by two days. Garfield kept strict account of this. He was on deck when we made the land, a dark and foggy night it was! nothing could be seen but the dimmest outline of a headland through the haze. I knew the place, I thought, and Garfield said he could smell land, fog or coal-tar.

This, it will be admitted, was reassuring. A school of merry porpoises that gambolled under the bows while we stood confidently in for the land, diving and crossing the bark's course in every direction, also guarded her from danger. I knew that so long as deep-sea porpoises kept with us we had nothing to fear of the ground. When the lookout cried, "Porpoises gone," we turned the bark's head off-shore, backed the main-tops'l, and sent out the "pigeon" (lead). A few grains of sand and one soft, delicate white shell were brought up out of fourteen fathoms of water. We had but to heed these warnings and guides, and our course would be tolerably clear, dense and all as the fog and darkness was.

The lead was kept constantly going as we sailed along in the intense darkness, till the headland of our port was visible through the haze of grey morning. What Garfield had smelled, I may mention, turned out to be coal-tar, a pot of which had been capsized on deck by the leadsman, in the night.

By daylight in the morning, April 29, we had found the inner entrance to Ilha Grande, and sailed into the harbour for the second time with this cargo of hay. It was still very foggy, and all day heavy gusts of wind came down through the gulches in the mountains, laden with fog and rain.

Two days later, the weather cleared up, and our friends began to come in. They found us there all right, anchored close under the highest mountain.

Eight days of sullen gloom and rain at this place; then brimstone, smoke, and fire turned on to us, and we were counted healthy enough to be admitted to *pratique* in Rio, where we arrived May 11th, putting one more day between ourselves and our friendly competitors, who finally arrived safe, all except one, the British bark *Dublin*. She was destroyed by fire between the two ports.

25

The crew was rescued by Captain Lunt, and brought safe into Rio next day.

At the fort entrance to the harbour of Rio we were again challenged and brought to, all standing, on the bar; the tide running like a mill race at the time brought the bark aback on her cables with a force, nearly cutting her down.

The *Aquidneck* it would seem had outsailed the telegram which should have preceded her; it was, nevertheless, my imperative duty to obey the orders of the port authorities which, however, should have been tempered with reason. It was easy for them in the fort to say, "Come to, or we'll sink you," but we in the bark, between two evils, came near being sunk by obeying the order.

Formerly, when a vessel was challenged at this fort, one, two or three shots, if necessary to bring her to, were fired, at a cost to the ship, if she were not American, of fifteen shillings for the first shot, thirty for the second, and sixty for the third; but, for American ships, the sixty shilling shot was fired first—Americans would always have the best!

After all the difficulties were cleared away, the tardy telegram received, and being again identified by the officers, we weighed anchor for the last time on this voyage, and went into our destined port, the spacious and charming harbour of Rio.

CHAPTER V

At Rio—Sail for Antonina with mixed cargo—A *pampeiro*—Ship on beam-ends—Cargo still more mixed—Topgallant-masts carried away—Arrive safely at Antonina.

THE cargo was at last delivered, and no one made ill over it. A change of rats also was made; at Rio those we brought in gave place to others from the Dom Pedro Docks where we moored. Fleas, too, skipped about in the hay as happy as larks, and nearly as big; and all the other live stock that we brought from Rosario, goodness knows of what kind and kith, arrived well and sound from over the water, notwithstanding the fumigations and fuss made at the quarantine.

Had the little microbes been with us indeed, the Brazilians would not have turned us away as they did, from the doors of an hospital! for they are neither a cruel nor cowardly people. To turn sickness away would be cruel and stupid, to say the least! What we were expelled for I have already explained.

After being so long in gloomy circumstances we felt like making the most of pleasant Rio! Therefore on the first fine day after being docked, we sallied out in quest of city adventure, and brought up first in Ouvidor— the Broadway of Rio, where my wife bought a tall hat, which I saw nights looming up like a dreadful stack of hay, the innocent cause of much trouble to me, and I declared, by all the great islands—in my dreams—that go back with it I would not, but would pitch it, first, into the sea.

I get nervous on the question of quarantines. I visit the famous Botanical Gardens with my family, and I

27

tremble with fear lest we are fumigated at some station on the way. However, our time at Rio is pleasantly spent in the main, and on the first day of June, we set sail once more for Paranagua and Antonina of pleasant recollections; partly laden with flour, kerosene, pitch, tar, rosin and wine, three pianos, I remember, and one steam engine and boiler, all as ballast; "freight free," so the bill of lading read, and further, that the ship should "not be responsible for leakage, breakage, or rust." This clause was well for the ship, as one of those wild *pampeiros* overtook her, on the voyage, throwing her violently on her beam-ends, and shaking the motley cargo into a confused and mixed-up mess. The vessel remaining tight, however, no very serious damage was done, and she righted herself after a while, but without her lofty topgallant-masts, which went with a crash at the first blast of the tempest.

This incident made a profound impression on Garfield. He happened to be on deck when the masts were carried away, but managed to scamper off without getting hurt. Whenever a vessel hove in sight after that having a broken spar or a torn sail, it was "a *pampeiroed* ship."

The storm, though short, was excessively severe, and swept over Paranagua and Antonina with unusual violence. The owner of the pianos, I was told, prayed for us, and regretted that his goods were not insured. But when they were landed, not much the worse for their tossing about, old Strichine, the owner (that was his name or near that, strychnine the boys called him, because his singing was worse than "rough on rats," they said, a bit of juvenile wit that the artist very sensibly let pass unheeded), declared that the ship was a good one, and that her captain was a good pilot; and as neither freight nor insurance had been paid, he and his wife would feast us on music; having learned that I especially was fond of it. They had screeched operas for a lifetime in Italy, but I didn't care for that. As arranged, therefore, I was on deck at the appointed time and place, to stay at all hazards.

The pianos, as I had fully expected, were fearfully out of tune—suffering, I should say, from the effects of seasickness!

So much so that I shall always believe this opportunity was seized upon by the artist to avenge the damage to his instruments, which, indeed, I could not avert, in the storm that we passed through. The good Strichine and his charming wife were astonished at the number of opera airs I could name. And they tried to persuade me to sing Il Trovatore; but concluding that damage enough had already been done, I refrained, that is, I refracted my song.

CHAPTER VI

Mutiny—Attempt at robbery and murder—Four against one —Two go down before a rifle—Order restored.

JULY 23rd, 1887, brings me to a sudden and shocking point in the history of the voyage that I fain would forget, but that will not be possible. Between the hours of 11 and 12 p.m. of this day I was called instantly to defend my life and all that is dear to a man.

The bark, anchored alone in the harbour of Antonina, was hid from the town in the darkness of a night that might well have covered the blackest of tragedies. My pirates thought their opportunity had surely come to capture the *Aquidneck*, and this they undertook to do. The ringleader of the gang was a burly scoundrel, whose boast was that he had "licked" both the mate and second mate of the last vessel he had sailed in, and had "busted the captain in the jaw" when they landed in Rio, where the vessel was bound, and where, of course, the captain had discharged him. It was there the villain shipped with me, in lieu of one of the Rosario gang who had been kindly taken in charge by the guard at Ilha Grande and brought to Rio to be tried before the American Consul for insubordination. Said he, one day when I urged him to make haste and help save the topsails in a squall, "Oh, I'm no soft-horn to be hurried!" It was the time the bark lost her topgallant-mast and was cast on her beam-ends on the voyage to Antonina, already told; it was, in fact, no time for loafing, and this braggart at a decisive word hurried aloft with the rest to do his duty. What I said to him was meant for earnest, and it cowed him. It is only

30

natural to think that he held a grudge against me forever after, and waited only for his opportunity; knowing, too, that I was the owner of the bark, and supposed
to have money. He was heard to say in a rum-mill a day
or two before the attack that he would find the ——
money and his life, too. His chum and bosom friend
had come pretty straight from Palermo penitentiary
at Buenos Aires when he shipped with me at Rosario.

It was no secret on board the bark that he had served
two years for robbing, and cutting a ranchman's throat
from ear to ear. These records, which each seemed to
glory in, were verified in both cases.

I met the captain afterwards who had been "busted
in the jaw"—Captain Roberts, of Baltimore, a quiet
gentleman, with no evil in his heart for any one, and a
man, like myself, well along in years.

Two of the gang, old Rosario hands, had served for
the lesser offence of robbery alone—they brought up
in the rear! The other two of my foremast hands—one a
very respectable Hollander, the other a little Japanese
sailor, a bright, young chap—had been robbed and
beaten by the four ruffians, and then threatened so that
they deserted to the forest instead of bringing a com-
plaint of the matter to me, for fear, as the Jap expressed
it afterwards, when there was no longer any danger,—
for fear the "la-la-long mans (thieves) would makee
killo mi!"

The ringleader bully had made unusual efforts to
create a row when I came on board early in the evening;
however, as he had evidently been drinking, I passed it
off as best I could for the natural consequence of rum,
and ordered him forward; instead of doing as he was
bid, when I turned to hand my wife to the cabin he
followed me threateningly to the break of the poop.
What struck me most, however, was the conduct of his

chum, who was sober, but in a very unusual, high, glee-
ful mood. It was knock-off time when I came along to
where he was seizing off the mizzen topgallant back-
stay, the last of the work of refitting the late *pampeiro*
damage; and the mate being elsewhere engaged, I gave
the usual order to quit work. "Knock off," I said to the
man, "and put away your tools. The bark's rigging
looks well," I added, "and if to-morrow turns out fine,
all will be finished"; whereupon the fellow laughed
impertinently in my face, repeating my words, "All
will be finished!" under his breath, adding, "before to-
morrow!" This was the first insult offered by the "Blood-
thirsty Tommy," who had committed murder only a
short time before; but I had been watched by the fellow,
with a cat-like eye at every turn.

The full significance of his words on this occasion
came up to me only next morning, when I saw him
lying on the deck with a murderous weapon in his hand!
I was not expecting a cowardly, night attack, nevertheless I kept my gun loaded. I went to sleep this night as
usual, forgetting the unpleasant episode as soon as my
head touched the pillow; but my wife, with finer in-
stincts, kept awake. It was well for us all that she did so.
Near midnight, my wife, who had heard the first foot-
step on the poop-deck, quietly wakened me, saying,
"We must get up, and look out for ourselves! Something is going wrong on deck; the boat tackle has been
let go with a great deal of noise, and —O! don't go that
way on deck. I heard some one on the cabin steps, and
heard whispering in the forward entry."

"You must have been dreaming," I said.

"No, indeed!" said she; "I have not been asleep yet;
don't go on deck by the forward companionway; they
are waiting there, I am sure, for I heard the creaking
of the loose step in the entry."

If my wife has not been dreaming, thought I, there can be no possible doubt of a plot.

Nothing justifies a visit on the poop-deck after working-hours, except a call to relieve sickness, or for some other emergency, and then secrecy or stealth is non-permissible.

It may be here explained to persons not familiar with ships, that the sailors' quarters are in the forward part of the ship where they (the sailors) are supposed to be found after working-hours, in port, coming never abaft the mainmast; hence the term "before the mast."

My first impulse was to step on deck in the usual way, but the earnest entreaties of my wife awoke me to a danger that should be investigated with caution. Arming myself, therefore, with a stout carbine repeater, with eight ball cartridges in the magazine, I stepped on deck abaft instead of forward, where evidently I had been expected. I stood rubbing my eyes for a moment, inuring them to the intense darkness, when a coarse voice roared down the forward companionway to me to come on deck. "Why don't ye come on deck like a man, and order yer men forid?" was the salute that I got, and was the first that I heard with my own ears, and it was enough. To tell the whole story in a word, I knew that I had to face a mutiny.

I could do no less than say: "Go forward there!"

"Yer there, are ye?" said the spokesman, as with an oath, he bounded toward me, cursing as he came.

Again I ordered him forward, saying, "I am armed, —if you come here I will shoot!" But I forbore to do so instantly, thinking to club him to the deck instead, for my carbine was a heavy one. I dealt him a blow as he came near, sufficient I thought, to fell an ox; but it had, apparently, no effect, and instantly he was inside of my guard. Then grasping me by the throat, he tried to

33

force me over the taffrail, and cried, exultingly, as he felt me give way under his brute strength, "Now, you damn fool, shoot!" at the same time drawing his knife to strike.

I could not speak, or even breathe, but my carbine spoke for me, and the ruffian fell with the knife in his hand which had been raised against me! Resolution had proved more than a match for brute force, for I then knew that not only my own life but also the lives of others depended on me at this moment. Nothing daunted, the rest came on, like hungry wolves. Again I cried, "Go forward!" But thinking, maybe, that my rifle was a single shooter, or that I could not load it so quickly, the order was disregarded.

"What if I don't go forward?" was "Bloody Tommy's" threatening question, adding, as he sprang toward me, "I've got this for you!" but fell instantly as he raised his hand; and there on the deck was ended his misadventure! and like the other he fell with the deadly knife in his hand. I was now all right. The dread of cold steel had left me when I freed myself from the first would-be assassin, and I only wondered how many more would persist in trying to take my life. But recollecting there were only two mutineers left, and that I had still six shots in the magazine of my rifle, and one already in the chamber, I stood ready with the hammer raised, and my finger on the trigger, confident that I would not be put down.

There was no further need of extreme measures, however, for order was now restored, though two of the assailants had skulked away in the dark.

How it was that I regained my advantage, after once losing it, I hardly know; but this I am certain of, that being down I was not to be spared. Then desperation took the place of fear, and I felt more than a match for

all that could come against me. I had no other than
serene feelings, however, and had no wish to pursue
the two pirates that fled.

Immediately after the second shot was fired, and I
found myself once more master of my bark, the remaining two came aft again, at my bidding this time,
and in an orderly manner, it may be believed.

It is idle to say what I would or would not have given
to have the calamity averted, or, in other words, to have
had a crew of sailors, instead of a gang of cut-throats.

However, when the climax came, I had but one
course to pursue; this I resolutely followed. A man will
defend himself and his family to the last, for life is sweet,
after all.

It was significant, the court thought afterwards, that
while my son had not had time to dress, they all had on
their boots except the one who fell last, and he was in
his socks, with no boots on. It was he who had waited
for me as I have already said, on the cabin steps that I
usually passed up and down on, but this time avoided.
Circumstantial evidence came up in abundance to
make the case perfectly clear to the authorities. There
are few who will care to hear more about a subject so
abhorrent to all, and I care less to write about it. I
would not have said this much, but for the enterprise
of a rising department clerk, who, seeing the importance
of telling to the world what he knew, and seeing also some
small emolument in the matter, was I believe prompted
to augment the consular dispatches, thus obliging me
to fight the battle over. However, not to be severe on
the poor clerk, I will only add that no indignities were
offered me by the authorities through all the strict
investigation that followed the tragedy.

The trial being for justice and not for my money the
case was soon finished.

I sincerely hope that I may never again encounter such as those who came from the jails to bring harm and sorrow in their wake.

The work of loading was finished soon after the calamity to my bark, and a Spanish sailing-master was engaged to take her to Montevideo; my son Victor going as flag captain.

I piloted the *Aquidneck* out of the harbour, and left her clear of the buoy, looking as neat and trim as sailor could wish to see. All the damage done by the late *pampeiro* had been repaired, new topgallant-masts rigged, and all made ataunto. I saw my handsome bark well clear of the dangers of the harbour limits, then in sorrow I left her and paddled back to the town, for I was on parole to appear, as I have said, for trial! That was the word; I can find no other name for it—let it stand!

CHAPTER VII

Join the bark at Montevideo—A good crew—Small-pox breaks out—Bear up for Maldonado and Flores—No aid—Death of sailors—To Montevideo in distress—Quarantine.

As soon as the case was over I posted on for Montevideo by steamer, where the bark had arrived only a few days ahead of me. I found her already stripped to a gantline though, preparatory to a long stay in port. I had given Victor strict orders to interfere in no way with the Spaniard, but to let him have full charge in nearly everything. I could have trusted the lad with full command, young as he was; but there was a strange crew of foreigners which might, as often happens, require maturer judgment to manage than to sail the vessel. As it proved, however, even the *cook* was in many ways a better man than the sailing-master.

Victor met me with a long face, and the sailors wore a quizzical look as I came over the vessel's side. One of them, in particular, whom I shall always remember, gave me a good-humoured greeting, along with his shake of the head, that told volumes; and next day was aloft, crossing yards, cheerfully enough. I found my Brazilian crew to be excellent sailors, and things on board the *Aquidneck* immediately began to assume a brighter appearance, aloft and alow.

Cargo was soon discharged, other cargo taken in, and the bark made ready for sea. My crew, I say, was a good one; but, poor fellows, they were doomed to trials—the worst within human experience, many of them giving up to grim death before the voyage was ended. Too often one bit of bad luck follows another. This rule

37

brought us in contact with one of these small officials at Montevideo, better adapted to home life; one of those knowing, perhaps, more than need a cowboy, but not enough for consul. This official, managing to get word to my crew that a change of master dissolved their contract, induced them to come on shore and claim pay for the whole voyage and passage home on a steamer besides, the same as though the bark had been sold.

What overwhelming troubles may come of having incompetent officials in places of trust, the sequel will show. This unwise, even stupid interference, was the indirect cause of the sufferings and deaths among the crew which followed.

I was able to show the consul and his clerk that sailors are always engaged for the ship, and never for the master, and that a change of master did not in any way affect their contract. However, I paid the crew off, and then left it to their option to re-ship or not, for they were all right, they had been led to do what they did, and I knew that they wanted to get home, and it was there that the bark was going, direct.

All signed the articles again, except one, a long-haired Andalusian, whom I would not have longer at any price. The wages remained the same as before, and all hands returned to their duty cheerful and contented—but pending the consul's decision (which, by the way, I decided for him), they had slept in a contagioned house, where, alas, they contracted small-pox of the worst type.

We were now homeward bound. All the "runaway rum" that could be held out by the most subtle crimps of Montevideo could not induce these sober Brazilian sailors to desert their ship.

These "crimps" are land-sharks who get the sailors drunk when they can, and then rob them of their advance money. The sailors are all paid in advance; sometimes they receive in this way most of their wages for the voyage, which they make after the money is spent, or wasted, or stolen.

We all know what working for dead horse means— sailors know too well its significance.

As sailing day drew near, a half-day liberty to each watch was asked for by the men, who wanted to make purchases for their friends and relatives at Paranagua. Permission to go on shore was readily granted, and I was rewarded by seeing every one return to his ship at the time promised, and every one sober. On the morrow, which was sailing day, every man was at his post and all sang "Cheerily, ho!" and were happy; all except one, who complained of slight chills and a fever, but said that he had been subject to this, and that with a dose of quinine he would soon be all right again.

It appeared a small matter. Two days later though, his chills turned to something which I knew less about. The next day, three more men went down with rigor in the spine, and at the base of the brain. I knew by this that small-pox was among us!

We bore up at once for Maldonado, which was the nearest port, the place spoken of in "Gulliver's Travels," though Gulliver, I think, is mistaken as to its identity and location, arriving there before a gathering storm that blew wet and cold from the east. Our signals of distress, asking for immediate medical aid were set and flew thirty-six hours before any one came to us; then a scared Yahoo (the country was still inhabited by Yahoos) in a boat rowed by two other animals, came aboard, and said, "Yes, your men have got small-pox." "*Vechega*," he called it, but I understand the lingo of the Yahoo very well, I could even speak a few words of it and comprehend the meanings. "*Vechega!*" he bellowed

39

to his mates alongside, and, turning to me, he said, in Yahoo: "You must leave the port at once," then jumping into his boat he hurried away, along with his scared companions.[1]

To leave a port in our condition was hard lines, but my perishing crew could get no succour at Maldonado, so we could do nothing but leave, if at all able to do so. We were indeed short-handed, but desperation lending a hand, the anchor was weighed and sufficient sail set on the bark to clear the inhospitable port. The wind blowing fair out of the harbour carried us away from the port toward Flores Island, for which we now headed in sore distress. A gale, long to be remembered, sprang suddenly up, stripping off our sails like autumn leaves, before the bark was three leagues from the place. We hadn't strength to clew up, so her sails were blown away, and she went flying before the mad tempest under bare poles. A snow-white sea-bird came for shelter from the storm, and poised on the deck to rest. The incident filled my sailors with awe; to them it was a portentous omen, and in distress they dragged them-

[1] In our discourse, Yahoo was spoken, but I write it in English because many of my readers would not understand the original. The signals that we used were made by universal code symbols. For example, two flags hoisted representing "P" "D" signified "want (or wants) immediate medical assistance." And so on, by hoists of two, three or four flags representing the consonants, our wants and wishes could be made known, each possessing the key to the code.

Our commercial code of signals is so invented and arranged that no matter what tongues may meet, perhaps those utterly incomprehensible by word of mouth, yet by these signs communications may be carried on with great facility. The whole system is so beautifully simple that a child of ordinary intelligence can understand it. Even the Yahoos were made to comprehend—when not colour-blind. And, lest they should forget their lesson, a gunboat is sent out every year or two, to fire it into them with cannon.

selves together and, prostrate before the bird, prayed the Holy Virgin to ask God to keep them from harm. The rain beat on us in torrents, as the bark tossed and reeled ahead, and day turned black as night. The gale was from E.S.E., and our course lay W.N.W. nearly, or nearly before it. I stood at the wheel with my shore clothes on, I remember, for I hadn't yet had time to change them for waterproofs; this of itself was small matter, but it reminds me now that I was busy with other concerns. I was always a good helmsman, and I took in hand now the steering of the bark in the storm —and I gave directions to Victor and the carpenter how to mix disinfectants for themselves, and medicines for the sick men. The medicine chest was fairly supplied.

Flores, when seen, was but a few ship's lengths away. Flashes of lightning revealed the low cliffs, amazingly near to us, and as the bark swept by with great speed, the roar of the breakers on the shore, heard above the din of the storm, told us of a danger to beware. The helm was then put down, and she came to under the lee of the island like a true, obedient thing.

Both anchors were let go, and all the chain paid out to both, to the bitter end, for the gale was now a hurricane. She walked away with her anchors for all that we could do, till, hooking a marine cable, one was carried away, and the other brought her head to the wind, and held her there trembling in the storm.

Anxious fear lest the second cable should break was on our minds through the night; but a greater danger was within the ship, that filled us all with alarm.

Two barks not far from us that night, with pilots on board, were lost, in trying to come through where the *Aquidneck*, without a pilot and with but three hands on deck to work her, came in. Their crews, with great difficulty, were rescued and then carried to Montevideo.

When all had been done that we three could do, a light was put in the rigging, that flickered in the gale and went out. Then wet, and lame, and weary, we fell down in our drenched clothes, to rest as we might—to sleep, or to listen to groans of our dying shipmates.

When daylight came (after this, the most dismal of all my nights at sea), our signals went up telling of the sad condition of the crew, and begging for medical assistance. Toward night the gale went down; but, as no boat came off, a gloom darker than midnight settled over the crew of the pest-ridden bark, and in dismay they again prayed to be spared to meet the loved ones awaiting them at home.

Our repeated signals, next day, brought the reply, "Stand in." *Carramba!* Why, we could hardly stand at all; much less could we get the bark underway, and beat in against wind and current. No one knew this better than they on the island, for my signals had told the whole story, and as we were only a mile and a half from the shore, the flags were distinctly made out. There was no doubt in our minds about that!

Late in the day, however, a barge came out to us, ill-manned and ill-managed by as scared a set of "galoots" as ever capsized a boat, or trembled at a shadow! The coxswain had more to say than the doctor, and the Yahoo—I forgot to mention that we were still in Yahoo-dom, but one would see that without this explanation —the Yahoo in the bow said more than both; and they all took a stiff pull from a bottle of *cachazza*,[1] the doctor having had the start, I should say, of at least one or two pulls before leaving the shore, insomuch as he appeared braver than the rest of the crew.

The doctor, having taken an extra horn or two, with

[1] This *cachazza* is said to be death to microbes, or even to larger worms; it will kill anything, in fact, except a Yahoo!

42

Dutch courage came on board, and brought with him a pound of sulphur, a pint of carbolic acid, and some barley—enough to feed a robin a few times, for all of which we were thankful indeed, our disinfectants being by this time nearly exhausted; then, glancing at the prostrate men, he hurried away, as the other had done at Maldonado. I asked what I should do with the dead through the night—bury them where we lay? "Oh, no, no!" cried the Yahoo in the bow; but the doctor pointed significantly to the water alongside! I knew what he meant!

That night we buried José, the sailor whose honest smile had welcomed me to my bark at Montevideo. I had ordered stones brought on deck, before dark, ostensibly to ballast the boat. I knew they would soon be wanted! About midnight, the cook called me in sore distress, saying that José was dying without confession!

So poor José was buried that night in the great River Plate! I listened to the solemn splash that told of one life ended, and its work done; but gloomy, and sad, and melancholy as the case was, I had to smile when the cook, not having well-secured the ballast, threw it over after his friend, exclaiming, "Good-bye, José, good-bye!" I added, "Good-bye, good shipmate, good-bye! I doubt not that you rest well!"

Next day, the signal from the shore was the same as the day before, "Stand in," in answer to my repeated call for help. By this time my men were demoralized and panic-stricken, and the poor fellows begged me, if the doctor would not try to cure them, to get a priest to confess them all. I saw a padre pacing the beach, and set flags asking him to come on board. No notice was taken of the signal, and we were now left entirely to ourselves.

After burying one more of the crew, we decided to

remain no longer at this terrible place. An English telegraph tender passing, outward-bound, caught up our
signals at that point, and kindly reported to her consul
at Maldonado, who wired it to Montevideo.

The wind blowing away from the shore, as may it
always blow when friend of mine nears that coast, we
determined to weigh anchor or slip cable without
further loss of time, feeling assured that by the telegraph
reports some one would be on the look-out for us, and
that the *Aquidneck* would be towed into port if the worst
should happen—if the rest of her crew went down.
Three of us weighed one anchor, with its ninety fathoms
of chain, the other had parted on the windlass in the
gale. The bark's prow was now turned toward Montevideo, the place we had so recently sailed from, full of
hope and pleasant anticipation; and here we were,
dejected and filled with misery, some of our number
already gone on that voyage which somehow seems so
far away.

At Montevideo, things were better. They *did* take my
remaining sick men out of the vessel, after two days'
delay; my agent procuring a tug, which towed them in
the ship's boat three hundred fathoms astern. In this
way they were taken to Flores Island, where, days and
days before, they had been refused admittance! They
were accompanied this time by an order from the governor of Montevideo, and at last were taken in. Two of
the cases were, by this time, in the favourable change.
But the poor old cook, who stood faithfully by me, and
would not desert his old shipmates, going with them to
the Island to care for them to the last, took the dread
disease, died of it, and was there buried, not far from
where he himself had buried his friend José, a short
time before. The death of this faithful man occurred on
the day that the bark finally sailed seaward, by the

44

Island. She was in sight from the hospital window when his phantom ship, that put out, carried him over the bar! His widow, at Paranagua, I was told, on learning the fate of her husband, died of grief.

The work of disinfecting the vessel, at Montevideo, after the sick were removed, was a source of speculation that was most elaborately carried on. Demijohns of carbolic acid were put on board, by the dozen, at $3.00 per demijohn, all diluted ready for use; and a *guardo* was put on board to use it up, which he did religiously over his own precious self, in my after-cabin, as far from the end of the ship where the danger was as he could get. Some one else disinfected *el proa*, not he! Abundant as the stuff was, I had to look sharp for enough to wash out forward while aft it was knee-deep almost, at three dollars a jar! The harpy that alighted on deck at Maldonado sent in his bill for one hundred dollars—I paid eighty.

The cost to me of all this trouble in money paid out, irrelevantly to mention, was over a thousand dollars. What it cost me in health and mental anxiety cannot be estimated by such value. Still, I was not the greatest sufferer. My hardest task was to come, you will believe, at the gathering up of the trinkets and other purchases which the crew had made, thoughtful of wife and child at home. All had to be burned, or spoiled with carbolic acid! A hat for the little boy here, a pair of boots for his mamma there, and many things for the *familia* all around—all had to be destroyed!

CHAPTER VIII

A new crew—Sail for Antonina—Load timber—Native canoes—
Loss of the *Aquidneck.*

AFTER all this sad trouble was over, a new crew was
shipped, and the *Aquidneck's* prow again turned
seaward. Passing out by Flores, soon after, we observed
the coast-guard searching, I learned, for a supposed
sunken bark, which had appeared between squalls in
the late gale with signals of distress set. I was satisfied
from the account that it was our bark which they had
seen in the gale, and the supposed flags were our tattered
sails, what there was left of them, streaming in the
storm. But we did not discourage the search, as it could
do no harm, and I thought that they might perhaps
find something else worth knowing about. This was the
day, as I have said, on which my faithful cook died,
while the bark was in sight from the window of his sick
ward. It was a bright, fine day to us. We cannot say
that it was otherwise than bright to him.

Breathing once more the fresh air of the sea, we set all
sail for Paranagua, passing the lights on the coast to
leave them flickering on the horizon, then soon out of
sight. Fine weather prevailed, but with much head
wind; still we progressed, and rarely a day passed but
something of the distance toward our port was gained.
One day, however, coming to an island, one that was
inhabited only by birds, we came to a stand, as if it were
impossible to go farther on the voyage; a spell seemed
to hang over us. I recognized the place as one that I
knew well; a very dear friend had stood by me on deck,

looking at this island, some years before. It was the last land that my friend ever saw. I would fain have sailed around it now, but a puff of fair wind coming sent us on our course for the time some leagues beyond. At sunset, though, this wind went down, and with the current we drifted back so much that by the next day we were farther off on the other side. However, fair wind coming again, we passed up inside, making thus the circuit of the island at last.

More or less favourable winds thenceforth filled our sails, till at last our destined port was gained.

The little town of Antonina, where my wife and Garfield had remained over during this voyage, twelve miles up the bay from Paranagua, soon after our arrival, was made alive with the noise of children marching to children's own music, my "Yawcob" heading the band with a brand-new ninety-cent organ, the most envied fellow of the whole crowd. Sorrows of the past took flight, or were locked in the closet at home, the fittest place for past misfortunes.

A truly hard voyage for us all was that to Montevideo! The survivors reached home after a while. Their features were terribly marked and disfigured; so much so that I did not know them till they accosted me when we met.

I look back with pleasure to the good character of my Brazilian sailors, regretting the more their hard luck and sad fate! We may meet again! *Quien sabe!*

Getting over all this sad business as best we could, we entered on the next venture, which was to purchase and load a cargo of the famous Brazilian wood. The *Aquidneck* was shifted to an arm of the bay, where she was moored under the lee of a virgin forest, twenty minutes' canoe ride from the village of Guarakasava, where she soon began to load.

The timber of this country, generally very heavy, is nevertheless hauled by hand to the water, where, lashed to canoes, it is floated to the ship.

These canoes, formed sometimes from mammoth trees, skilfully shaped and dug out with care, are at once the carriage and *cariole* of the family to the *citio*, or the rice to mill. Roads are hardly known where the canoe is available; men, women, and children are consequently alike, skilled in the art of canoeing to perfection, almost. There are no carriages to speak of in such places, even a saddle horse about the waterfront is a *rara avis*. There was, indeed, one horse at Guarakasava—the owner of it was very conspicuous.

The family canoe just spoken of, has the capacity, often, of several tons, is handsomely decorated with carvings along the topsides, and is painted, as the "Geordie" would say, "in none o' your gaudy colours, but in good plain red or blue"—sometimes, however, they are painted green.

The cost of these handsome canoes are, say, from $250 down in price and size, from the grand turnout to the one-man craft which may be purchased for five milreis ($2.50).

From the greatest to the smallest they are cared for with almost an affectionate care, and are made to last many years.

One thing else which even the poorest Brazilian thinks much of is his affectionate wife who literally and figuratively is often in the same boat with her husband, pulling against the stream. Family ties are strong in Brazil and the sweet flower of friendship thrives in its sunny clime. The system of land and sea breezes prevail on the coast from Cape Frio to Saint Catherine with great regularity most of the year; the sail is therefore used to good advantage by the almost amphibious inhabitants along the coast who love the water and take to it like ducks and natural born sailors.

The wind falling light they propel their canoes by paddle or long pole with equal facility. The occupants standing, in the smaller ones, force them along at a great speed. The larger ones, when the wind does not serve, are pulled by banks of oars which are fastened to stout pegs in the gunwail with grummits, that fit loosely over the oars so as to allow them free play in the hand of the waterman.

Curling the water with fine, shapely prows as they dart over the smooth waters of the bays and rivers, these canoes present a picture of unrivalled skill and grace.

I find the following entry in my diary made near the close of transactions at Guarakasava which in the truthful word of an historian I am bound to record, if only to show my prevailing high opinion of the natives while I was among them:—

GUARAKASAVA, Dec. 20th.

Heretofore I have doted on native Brazilian honesty as well as national seamanship and skill in canoes but my dream of a perfect paradise is now unsettled forever. I find, alas! that even here the fall of Adam is felt: Taking in some long poles to-day the negro tallyman persisted in counting twice the same pole. When the first end entered the port it was "*umo*" (one); when the last end disappeared into the ship he would sing out "*does*" (two).

I had no serious difficulty over the matter, but left Guarakasava with that hurt feeling which comes of being over persuaded that one and one make four.

We spent Christmas of 1887 at Guarakasava. The bark was loaded soon after, and when proceeding across the bay, where currents and wind caught her foul near a dangerous sand bar, she misstayed and went on the strand. The anchor was let go to club her. It wouldn't hold in the treacherous sands; so she dragged and stranded broadside on, where, open to the sea, a strong swell came in that raked her fore and aft for three days, the waves dashing over her groaning hull the while till at last her back was broke and—why not add heart as well! for she lay now undone. After twenty-five years of good service the *Aquidneck* here ended her days!

I had myself carried load on load, but alas! I could not carry a mountain; and was now at the end where my best skill and energy could not avail. What was to be done? What could be done? We had indeed the appearance of shipwrecked people, away, too, from home.

This was no time to weep, for the lives of all the crew were saved; neither was it a time to laugh, for our loss was great.

But the sea calmed down, and I sold the wreck, which floated off at the end of the storm. And after paying the crew their wages out of the proceeds had a moiety left for myself and family—a small sum.

Then I began to look about for the future, and for means of escape from exile. The crew (foreign) found shipping for Montevideo, where they had joined the *Aquidneck,* in lieu of the stricken Brazilian sailors. But for myself and family this outlet was hardly available, even if we had cared to go farther from home,—which was the least of our thoughts; and there were no vessels coming our way.

CHAPTER IX

The building of the *Liberdade*.

Away, away, no cloud is lowering o'er us
Freely now we stem the wave;
Hoist, hoist all sail, before us
Hope's beacon shines to cheer the brave.
—*Masaniello.*

WHEN all had been saved from the wreck that was worth saving, or that could be saved, we found ourselves still in the possession of some goods soon to become of great value to us, especially my compass and charts which, though much damaged, were yet serviceable and suggested practical usefulness; and the chronometer being found intact, my course was no longer undecided, my wife and sons agreeing with what I thought best.

The plan, in a word, was this: We could not beg our way, neither would we sit idle among the natives. We found that it would require more courage to remain in the far-off country than to return home in a boat, which then we concluded to build and for that purpose.[1]

My son Victor, with much pride and sympathy, entered heartily into the plan, which promised a speedy return home. He bent his energies in a practical direction, working on the boat like an old builder.

Before entering on the project, however, all responsibilities were considered. Swift ocean currents around capes and coral reefs were taken into account; and

[1] This alternative I was obliged to accept, or bring my family home as paupers, for my wealth was gone—need I explain more? This explanation has been forced from me.

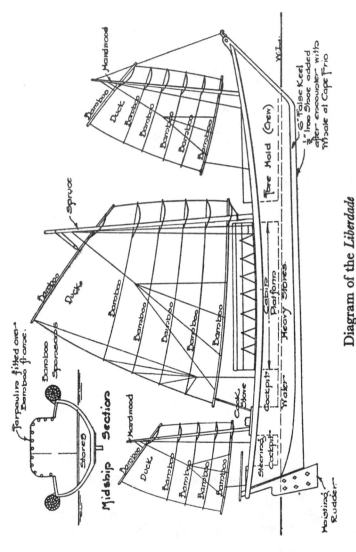

Diagram of the *Liberdade*

(Length 35 ft. beam 7½ ft., draught 2½ ft. weight 6 tons.)

52

above all else to be called dangerous we knew would be the fierce tropical storms which surely we would encounter.

But a boat should be built stout and strong, we all said, one in which we should not be afraid to trust our lives even in the storm.

And with the advantage of experience in ships and boats of various sizes and in many seas, I turned to the work of constructing, according to my judgment and means, a craft which would be best adapted to all weathers and all circumstances. My family with sympathetic strength pulling hard in the same direction.

Seaworthiness was to be the first and most prominent feature in our microscopic ship; next to this good quality she should sail well; at least before free winds. We counted on favourable winds; and so they were experienced the greater part of the voyage that soon followed.

Long exposures and many and severe disappointments by this time, I found, ha told on health and nerve, through long quarantines, expensive fumigations, and ruinous doctors' visits, which had swept my dollars into hands other than mine. However, with still a "shot in the locker," and with some feelings of our own in the matter of how we should get home, I say, we set to work with tools saved from the wreck—a meagre kit—and soon found ourselves in command of another ship, which I will describe the building of, also the dimensions and the model and rig, first naming the tools with which it was made.

To begin with, we had an axe, an adze, and two saws, one $\frac{1}{2}$-inch auger, one $\frac{6}{8}$ and one $\frac{3}{8}$ auger-bit; two large sail-needles, which we converted into nailing bits; one roper, that answered for a punch; and, most precious of all, a file that we found in an old sail-bag washed up on the beach. A square we readily made.

Two splints of bamboo wood served as compasses. Charcoal, pounded as fine as flour and mixed in water, took the place of chalk for the line; the latter we had on hand. In cases where holes larger than the $\frac{6}{8}$ bit were required, a piece of small jack-stay iron was heated, and with this we could burn a hole to any size required. So we had, after all, quite a kit to go on with. Clamps, such as are used by boat builders, we had not, but made substitutes from the crooked guava tree and from *massaranduba* wood.

Trees from the neighbouring forest were felled when the timber from the wrecked cargo would not answer. Some of these woods that we sought for special purposes had queer sounding names, such as *arregebah, guanandee, batetenandinglastampai*, etc. This latter we did not use the saw upon at all, it being very hard, but hewed it with the axe, bearing in mind that we had but one file, whereas for the edged tools we had but to go down to a brook hard by to find stones in abundance suitable to sharpen them on.

The many hindrances encountered in the building of the boat will not be recounted here. Among the least was a jungle fever, from which we suffered considerably. But all that and all other obstacles vanished at last, or became less, before a new energy which grew apace with the boat, and the building of the craft went rapidly forward. There was no short day system, but we rested on the Sabbath, or surveyed what we had done through the week, and made calculations of what and how to strike on the coming week.

The unskilled part of the labour, such as sawing the cedar planks, of which she was mostly made, was done by the natives, who saw in a rough fashion, always leaving much planing and straightening to be done, in order to adjust the timber to a suitable shape. The planks for the bottom were of ironwood, $1\frac{1}{4} \times 10$ inches. For the sides and top red cedar was used, each plank, with the exception of two, reaching the whole length of the boat. This arrangement of exceedingly heavy wood in the bottom, and the light on top, contributed much to the stability of the craft.

The ironwood was heavy as stone, while the cedar, being light and elastic, lent buoyancy and suppleness, all that we could wish for.

The fastenings we gathered up in various places, some from the bulwarks of the wreck, some from the hinges of doors and skylights, and some were made from the ship's metal sheathing, which the natives melted and cast into nails. Pure copper nails, also, were procured from the natives, some ten *kilos*, for which I paid in copper coins, at the rate of two *kilos* of coin for one *kilo* of nails. The same kind of coins, called *dumps*, cut into diamond-shaped pieces, with holes punched through them, entered into the fastenings as burrs for the nails. A number of small eyebolts from the spanker-boom of the wreck were turned to account for lashing bolts in the deck of the new vessel. The nails, when too long, were cut to the required length, taking care that the ends which were cut off should not be wasted, but remelted, along with the metal sheathing, into other nails.

Some carriage bolts, with nuts, which I found in the country, came in very handy; these I adjusted to the required length, when too long, by slipping on blocks of wood of the required thickness to take up the surplus length, putting the block, of course, on the inside, and counter-sinking the nut flush with the planks on the outside; then screwing from the inside outward, they were drawn together, and there held as in a vice, the planks being put together "lap-streak" fashion, which without doubt is the strongest way to build a boat.

These screw-bolts, seventy in number, as well as the copper nails, cost us dearly, but wooden pegs, with which also she was fastened, cost only the labour of being made. The lashings, too, that we used here and there about the frame of the cabin, cost next to nothing, being made from the fibrous bark of trees, which could be had in abundance by the stripping of it off. So, taking it by and large, our materials were not expensive, the principal item being the timber, which cost about three cents per superficial foot, sawed or hewed. Rosewood, ironwood, cedar or mahogany, were all about the same price and very little in advance of common wood; so of course we selected always the best, the labour of shaping being least, sometimes, where the best materials were used.

These various timbers and fastenings, put together as best we could shape and join them, made a craft sufficiently strong and seaworthy to withstand all the buffetings on the main upon which, in due course, she was launched.

The hull being completed, by various other contrivances and makeshifts in which, sometimes, the "wooden blacksmith" was called in to assist, and the mother of invention also lending a hand, fixtures were made which served as well on the voyage as though made in a dockyard and at great cost.

My builders baulked at nothing, and on the 13th day of May, the day on which the slaves of Brazil were set free, our craft was launched, and was named *Liberdade* (Liberty).

Her dimensions being—35 feet in length over all, 7½ feet breadth of beam, and 3 feet depth of hold. Who shall say that she was not large enough?

Her model I got from my recollections of Cape Ann dories and from a photo of a very elegant Japanese *sampan* which I had before me on the spot, so, as it might be expected, when finished she resembled both types of vessel in some degree.

Her rig was the Chinese *sampan* style, which is, I consider, the most convenient boat rig in the whole world.

This was the boat, or canoe I prefer to call it, in which we purposed to sail for North America and home. Each one had been busy during the construction and past misfortunes had all been forgotten. Madam had made the sails—and very good sails they were, too!

Victor, the carpenter, ropemaker, and general roustabout had performed his part. Our little man, Garfield, too, had found employment in holding the hammer to clinch the nails and giving much advice on the coming voyage. All were busy, I say, and no one had given a thought of what we were about to encounter from the port officials farther up the coast; it was pretended by them that a passport could not be granted to so small a craft to go on so long a voyage as the contemplated one to North America.

Then fever returned to the writer and the constructor of the little craft, and I was forced to go to bed, remaining there three days. Finally, it came to my mind that in part of a medicine chest, which had been saved from the wreck, was stored some *arsenicum*, I think it is called. Of this I took several doses (small ones at first, you may be sure), and the good effect of the deadly poison on the malaria in my system was soon felt trickling through my veins. Increasing the doses somewhat, I could perceive the beneficial effect hour by hour, and in a few days I had quite recovered from the malady. Absurd as it was to have the judgment of sailors set on by pollywog navigators, we had still to submit, the pollywogs being numerous.

About this time—as the astrologers say—a messenger came down from the *Alfandega* (Custom House), asking me to repair thither at midday on the morrow. This filled me with alarm. True, the messenger has delivered his message in the politest possible manner, but that signified nothing, since Brazilians are always polite. This thing, small as it seems now, came near sending me back to the fever.

What had I done?

I went up next day, after having nightmare badly all night, prepared to say that I wouldn't do it again! The kind administrator I found, upon presenting myself at his office, had no fault to charge me with; but had a good word, instead. "The little *Liberdade*," he observed, had attracted the notice of his people and his own curiosity, as being "a handsome and well-built craft." This and many other flattering expressions were vented, at which I affected surprise, but secretly said, "I think you are right, sir, and you have good taste, too, if you are a customs officer."

The drift of this flattery, to make a long story short, was to have me build a boat for the *Alfandega*, or, his government not allowing money to build new—pointing to one which certainly would require new keel, planks, ribs, stem, and stern-post—"could I not repair one?"

To this proposition I begged time to consider. Flattering as the officer's words were, and backed by the offer of liberal pay, so long as the boat could be "repaired," I still had no mind to remain in the hot country, and risk getting the fever again. But there was the old hitch to be gotten over; namely, the passport, on which, we thought, depended our sailing.

However, to expedite matters, a fishing licence was

hit upon, and I wondered why I had not thought of that before, having been, once upon a time, a fisherman myself. Heading thence on a new diplomatic course, I commenced to fit ostensibly for a fishing voyage. To this end, a fishing net was made, which would be a good thing to have, anyway. Then hooks and lines were rigged and a cable made. This cable, or rope, was formed from vines that grow very long on the sand-banks just above tide water, several of which twisted together make a very serviceable rope, then being light and elastic, it is especially adapted for a boat anchor rope, or for the storm drag. Ninety fathoms of this rope was made for us by the natives, for the sum of ten milreis ($5.00).

The anchor came of itself almost. I had made a wooden one from heavy sinking timber, but a stalwart ranchman coming along, one day, brought a boat anchor with him which, he said, had been used by his slaves as a pot-hook. "But now that they are free and away," said he, "I have no further use for the crooked thing." A sewing-machine, which had served to stitch the sails together, was coveted by him, and was of no further use to us; in exchange for this the prized anchor was readily secured, the owner of it leaving us some boot into the bargain. Things working thus in our favour, the wooden anchor was stowed away to be kept as a spare bower.

These arrangements completed, our craft took on the appearance of a fishing smack, and I began to feel somewhat in my old element, with no fear of the lack of ways and means when we should arrive on our own coast, where I knew of fishing banks. And a document which translated read: "A licence to catch fish inside and outside of the bar" was readily granted by the port authorities.

"How far outside the bar may this carry us?" I asked.
"*Quien sabe!*" said the officer. (Literally translated, "Who knows?" but in Spanish or Portuguese used for, "Nobody knows, or, I don't care.")

"Adieu, señor," said the polite official; "we will meet in heaven!"

This meant you can go since you insist upon it, but I must not officially know of it; and you will probably go to the bottom. In this he and many others were mistaken.

Having the necessary document now in our possession, we commenced to take in stores for the voyage, as follows: Sea-biscuits, 120 lbs.; flour, 25 lbs.; sugar, 30 lbs.; coffee, 9 lbs., which, roasted black and pounded fine as wheaten flour, was equal to double the amount as prepared in North America, and afforded us a much more delicious cup.

Of tea we had 3 lbs.; pork, 20 lbs.; dried beef, 100 lbs.; *baccalao secca* (dried codfish), 20 lbs.; 2 bottles of honey, 200 oranges, 6 bunches of bananas, 120 gallons of water; also a small basket of yams, and a dozen sticks of sugar-cane, by way of vegetables.

Our medicine chest contained Brazil nuts, pepper, and cinnamon; no other medicines or condiments were required on the voyage, except table salt, which we also had.

One musket and a carbine—which had already stood us in good stead—together with ammunition and three cutlasses were stowed away for last use, to be used, nevertheless, in case of necessity.

The light goods I stowed in the ends of the canoe, the heavier in the middle and along the bottom, thus economizing space and lending to the stability of the canoe. Over the top of the midship stores a floor was made, which, housed over by a tarpaulin roof reaching three feet above the deck of the canoe, supported by a frame of bamboo, gave us sitting space of four feet from the floor to the roof, and twelve feet long amidships. This arrangement of cabin in the centre gave my passengers a berth where the least motion would be felt; even this is saying but little, for best we could do to avoid it we had still to accept much tossing from the waves.

Precautionary measures were taken in everything, so far as our resources and skill could reach. The springy and buoyant bamboo was used wherever stick of any kind was required, such as the frame and braces for the cabin, yards for the sails, and, finally, for guard on her top sides, making the canoe altogether a self-righting one, in case of a capsize. Each joint in the bamboo was an air-chamber of several pounds buoyant capacity, and we had a thousand joints.

The most important of our stores, particularly the flour, bread, and coffee, were hermetically sealed, so that if actually turned over at sea, our craft would not only right herself, but would bring her stores right side up, in good order, and it then would be only a question of baling her out, and of setting her again on her course, when we would come on as right as ever. As it turned out, however, no such trial or mishap awaited us.

While the possibility of many and strange occurrences was felt by all of us, the danger which loomed most in little Garfield's mind was that of the sharks.

A fine specimen was captured on the voyage, showing five rows of pearly teeth, as sharp as lances.

Some of these monsters, it is said, have nine rows of teeth; that they are always hungry is admitted by sailors of great experience.

How it is that sailors can go in bathing, as they often do, in the face of a danger so terrible, is past my comprehension. Their business is to face danger, to be sure, but this is a needless exposure, for which the penalty is sometimes a life. The second mate of a bark on the coast of Cuba, not long ago, was bitten in twain, and the portions swallowed whole by a monster shark that he had tempted in this way. The shark was captured soon after, and the poor fellow's remains taken out of the revolting maw.

Leaving the sharks where they are, I gladly return to the voyage of the *Liberdade*.

The *Liberdade*

CHAPTER X

Across the bar—The run to Santos—Tow to Rio by the steamship
—At Rio.

THE efficiency of our canoe was soon discovered: On
the 24th of June, after having sailed about the bay
some few days to temper our feelings to the new craft,
and shake things into place, we crossed the bar and
stood out to sea, while six vessels lay inside "bar-
bound," that is to say by their pilots it was thought
too rough to venture out, and they, the pilots, stood on
the point as we put out to sea, crossing themselves in
our behalf, and shouting that the bar was *crudo*. But
the *Liberdade* stood on her course, the crew never
regretting it.

The wind from the sou'west at the time was the
moderating side of a *pampeiro* which had brought in a
heavy swell from the ocean, that broke and thundered
on the bar with deafening roar and grand display of
majestic effort.

But our little ship bounded through the breakers like
a fish—as natural to the elements, and as free!

Of all the seas that broke furiously about her that day,
often standing her on end, not one swept over or even
boarded her, and she finally came through the storm of
breakers in triumph. Then squaring away before the
wind she spread her willing sails, and flew onward like
a bird.

It required confidence and some courage to face the
first storm in so small a bark, after having been years in
large ships; but it would have required more courage
than was possessed by any of us to turn back, since
thoughts of home had taken hold on our minds.

Then, too, the old boating trick came back fresh to me, the love of the thing itself gaining on me as the little ship stood out: and my crew with one voice said: "Go on." The heavy South Atlantic swell rolling in upon the coast, as we sped along, toppled over when it reached the ten fathom line, and broke into roaring combers, which forbade our nearer approach to the land.

Evidently, our safest course was away from the shore, and out where the swelling seas, though grand, were regular, and raced under our little craft that danced like a mite on the ocean as she drove forward. In twenty-four hours from the time Paranagua bar was crossed we were up with Santos Heads, a run of 150 miles.

A squall of wind burst on us through a gulch, as we swept round the Heads, tearing our sails into shreds, and sending us into Santos under bare poles.

Chancing then upon an old friend, the mail steamship *Finance*, Capt. Baker, about to sail for Rio, the end of a friendly line was extended to us, and we were towed by the stout steamer toward Rio, the next day, as fast as we could wish to go. My wife and youngest sailor took passage on the steamer, while Victor remained in the canoe with me, and stood by with axe in hand, to cut the tow-line, if the case should require it—and I steered.

"Look out," said Baker, as the steamer began to move ahead, "look out that I don't snake that canoe out from under you."

"Go on with your mails, Baker," was all I could say, "don't blow up your ship with my wife and son on board, and I will look out for the packet on the other end of the rope."

Baker opened her up to thirteen knots, but the *Liberdade* held on!

64

The line that we towed with was $1\frac{1}{3}$ inches in diameter, by ninety fathoms long. This, at times when the steamer surged over seas, leaving the canoe on the opposite side of a wave astern, would become as taut as a harp-string. At other times it would slacken and sink limp in a bight, under the forefoot, but only for a moment, however, when the steamer's next great plunge ahead would snap it taut again, pulling us along with a heavy, trembling jerk. Under the circumstances, straight steering was imperative, for a sheer to port or starboard would have finished the career of the *Liberdade*, by sending her under the sea. Therefore, the trick of twenty hours fell to me—the oldest and most experienced helmsman. But I was all right and not over-fatigued until Baker cast oil upon the "troubled waters." I soon got tired of that.

Victor was under the canvas covering, with the axe still in hand, ready to cut the line which was so arranged that he could reach it from within, and cut instantly, if by mischance the canoe should take a sheer.

I was afraid that the lad would become sleepy, and putting his head "under his wing" for a nap, would forget his post, but my frequent cry, "Stand by there, Victor," found him always on hand, though complaining somewhat of the dizzy motion.

Heavy sprays dashed over me at the helm, which, however, seeming to wash away the sulphur and brimstone smoke of many a quarantine, brought enjoyment to my mind.

Confused waves rose about us, high and dangerous—often high above the gunwale of the canoe—but her shapely curves balanced her well, and she rode over them all in safety.

This canoe ride was thrilling and satisfactory to us all. It proved beyond a doubt that we had in this little craft a most extraordinary sea-boat, for the tow was a thorough test of her seaworthiness.

The captain of the steamer ordered oil cast over from time to time, relieving us of much spray and sloppy motion, but adding to discomforts of taste to me at the helm, for much of the oil blew over me and in my face. Said the captain to one of his mates (an old whaler by the way, and whalers for some unaccountable reason have never too much regard for a poor merchantman), "Mr. Smith."

"Aye, aye, sir," answered old Smith.

"Mr. Smith, hoist out that oil."

"Aye, aye, sir," said the old "blubberhunter," in high glee, as he went about it with alacrity, and in less than five minutes from the time the order was given, I was smothering in grease and our boat was oiled from keel to truck.

"She's all right now," said Smith.

"That's all right," said Baker, but I thought it all wrong. The wind, meanwhile, was in our teeth and before we crossed Rio bar I had swallowed enough oil to cure any amount of consumption.

Baker, I have heard, said he wouldn't care much if he should "drown Slocum." But I was all right so long as the canoe didn't sheer, and we arrived at Rio safe and sound after the most exciting boat-ride of my life. I was bound not to cut the line that towed us so well; and I knew that Baker wouldn't let it go, for it was his rope.

I found at Rio that my fishing licence could be exchanged for a pass of greater import. This document had to be procured through the office of the Minister of Marine.

Many a smart linguist was ready to use his influence on my behalf with the above-named high official; but I

found at the end of a month that I was making headway about as fast as a Dutch galliot in a head sea after
the wind had subsided. Our worthy Consul, General
H. Clay Armstrong, gave me a hint of what the difficulty was and how to obviate it. I then went about the
business myself as I should have done at first, and I
found those at the various departments who were willing to help me without the intervention of outside
"influence."

Commander Marquis of the Brazilian navy recommended me to His Excellency, the Minister of Marine,
"out of regard," he said, "for American seamen," and
when the new document came it was *"Passe Especial,"*
and had on it *a seal as big as a soup plate.* A port naval
officer then presented me to the good *Administradore,*
who also gave me a *passe especial,* with the seal of the
Alfandega.

I had now only to procure a bill of health, when I
should have papers enough for a man-o'-war. Rio being
considered a healthy place, this was readily granted,
making our equipment complete.

I met here our minister whose office, with other
duties, is to keep a weather-eye lifting in the interest of
that orphan, the American ship—alas, my poor relation! Said he, "Captain, if your *Liberdade* be as good as
your papers" (documents given me by the Brazilian
officials), "you may get there all right"; adding, "well,
if the boat ever reaches home she will be a great
curiosity," the meaning of which, I could readily infer,
was, "and your chances for a snap in a dime museum
will be good." This, after many years of experience as
an American shipmaster, and also shipowner, in a
moderate way, was interesting encouragement. By our
Brazilian friends, however, the voyage was looked upon
as a success already achieved.

The utmost confidence [said the "Journal Opiz," of Rio], is placed in the cool-headed, audacious American mariner, and we expect in a short time to hear proclaimed in all of the journals of the Old and New World the safe arrival of this wonderful little craft at her destination, ourselves taking part in the glory. (Temos confianca na pericia e sangue frio do audaciauso marinhero Americano por isso esperamos que dentro em pouco tempo veremos o seu nome proclamado por todos os jornaes do velho e novo mundo. A nos tambem cabera parte da gloria.)

With these and like kind expressions from all of our *friends*, we took leave of Rio, sailing on the morning of July 23rd, 1888.

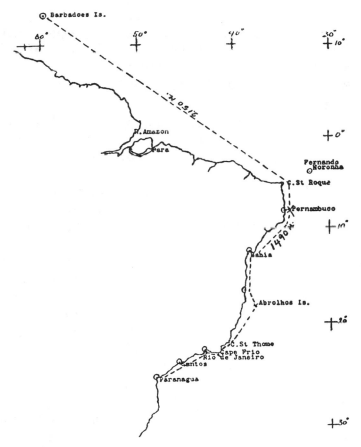

Course of the *Liberdade* from Paranagua to Barbadoes

CHAPTER XI

Sail from Rio—Anchor at Cape Frio—Encounter with a whale—
Sunken treasure—The schoolmaster—The merchant—The
good people at the village—A pleasant visit.

JULY 23rd, 1888, was the day, as I have said, on which
we sailed from Rio de Janeiro.

Meeting with head winds and light withal, through
the day we made but little progress; and finally, when
night came on, we anchored twenty miles east of Rio
Heads, near the shore. Long, rolling seas rocked us as
they raced by, then, dashing their great bodies against
defying rocks, made music by which we slept that night.
But a trouble unthought of before came up in Garfield's
mind before going to his bunk; "Mamma," cried he, as
our little bark rose and fell on the heavy waves, tumbling the young sailor about from side to side in the
small quarters while he knelt seriously at his evening
devotion, "mamma, this boat isn't big enough to pray
in!" But this difficulty was gotten over in time, and
Garfield learned to watch as well as to pray on the
voyage, and full of faith that all would be well, laid him
down nights and slept as restfully as any Christian on
sea or land.

By daylight of the second day we were again underweigh, beating to the eastward against the old head wind
and head sea. On the following night we kept her at it,
and the next day made Cape Frio where we anchored
near the entrance to a good harbour.

Time from Rio, two days; distance, 70 miles.

The wind and tide being adverse, compelled us to
wait outside for a favourable change. While comfort-

ably anchored at this place, a huge whale, nosing about, came up under the canoe, giving us a toss and a great scare. We were at dinner when it happened. The meal, it is needless to say, was finished without dessert. The great sea animal—fifty to sixty feet long—circling around our small craft, looked terribly big. He was so close to me twice, as he swam round and round the canoe, that I could have touched him either time with a paddle. His flukes stirring the water like a steamer propeller appeared alarmingly close and powerful!— and what an ugly mouth the monster had! Well, we expected instant annihilation. The fate of the stout whale-ship *Essex* came vividly before me. The voyage of the *Liberdade*, I thought, was about ended, and I looked about for pieces of bamboo on which to land my wife and family. Just then, however, to the infinite relief of all of us, the leviathan moved off, without doing us much harm, having felt satisfied, perhaps, that we had no Jonah on board.

We lost an anchor through the incident, and received some small damage to the keel, but no other injury was done—even this, I believe, upon second thought, was unintentional—done in playfulness only! "A shark can take a joke," it is said, and crack one too, but for broad, rippling humour the whale has no equal.

"If this be a sample of our adventures in the begin- ning," thought I, "we shall have enough and to spare by the end of the voyage." A visit from this quarter had not been counted on; but Sancho Panza says, "When least aware starts the hare," which in our case, by the by, was a great whale!

When our breath came back and the hair on our heads settled to a normal level, we set sail, and dodged about under the lee of the cape till a cove, with a very enticing sand beach at the head of it, opened before us, some three miles northwest of where we lost the anchor in the remarkable adventure with the whale. The "spare bower" was soon bent to the cable. Then we stood in and anchored near a cliff, over which was a goat-path leading in the direction of a small fishing village, about a mile away. Sheering the boat in to the rocky side of the cove which was steep to, we leaped out, warp in hand, and made fast to a boulder above the tidal flow, then, scrambling over the cliff, we repaired to the village, first improvising a spare anchor from three sticks and a stone which answered the purpose quite well.

Judging at once that we were strangers the villagers came out to meet us, and made a stir at home to entertain us in the most hospitable manner, after the custom of the country, and with the villagers was a gentleman from Canada, a Mr. Newkirk, who, as we learned, was engaged, when the sea was smooth, in recovering treasure that was lost near the cape in the British warship *Thetis*, which was wrecked there in 1830. The treasure, some millions in silver coins and gold in bars, from Peru for England, was dumped in the cove, which has since taken the name of the ship that bore it there and, as I have said, came to grief in that place which is on the west shore near the end of the cape.

Some of the coins were given to us to be treasured as souvenirs of the pleasant visit. We found in Mr. Newkirk a versatile, roving genius; he had been a schoolmaster at home, captain of a lake schooner once, had practised medicine, and preached some, I think; and what else I do not know. He had tried many things for a living, but, like the proverbial moving stone had failed to accumulate. "Matters," said the Canadian, "were getting worse and worse even, till finally to keep my head above water I was forced to go under the sea," and he had struck it rich, it would seem, if gold being brought in by the boat-load was any sign. This man of many adventures still spoke like a youngster; no one had told him that he was growing old. He talked of going home, as soon as the balance of the treasure was secured, "just to see his dear old mother," who, by the way, was seventy-four years old when he left home, some twenty years before. Since his last news from home, nearly two decades had gone by. He was "the youngest of a family of eighteen children, all living," he said, "though," added he, "our family came near being made one less yesterday, by a whale which I thought would eat my boat, diving-bell, crew, money and all, as he came toward us, with open mouth. By a back stroke of the oars, however, we managed to cheat him out of his dinner, if that was what he was after, and I think it was, but here I am!" he cried, "all right!" and might have added, "wealthy after all."

After hearing the diver's story, I related in Portuguese our own adventure of the same day, and probably with the same whale, the monster having gone in the direction of the diver's boat. The astonishment of the listeners was great; but when they learned of our intended voyage to *America do Norte*, they crossed themselves and asked God to lend us grace!

"Is North America near New York?" asked the village merchant, who owned all the boats and nets of the place.

"Why, America is *in* New York," answered the ex-schoolmaster.

"I thought so," said the self-satisfied merchant. And no doubt he thought some of us very stupid, or rude, or both, but in spite of manners I had to smile at the assuring air of the Canadian.

"Why did you not answer him correctly?" I asked of the ex-schoolmaster.

"I answered him," said Newkirk, "according to his folly. Had I corrected his rusty geography before these simple, impoverished fishermen, he would not soon forgive me; and as for the rest of the poor souls here, the knowledge would do them but little good."

I may mention that in this out-of-the-way place there were no schools, and except the little knowledge gained in their church, from the catechism, and from the fumbling of beads, they were the most innocent of this world's scheme, of any people I ever met. But they seemed to know all about heaven, and were, no doubt, happy.

After the brief, friendly chat that we had, coffee was passed around, the probabilities of the *Liberdade's* voyage discussed, and the crew cautioned against the dangers of the *balaena* (whale), which were numerous along the coast, and vicious at that season of the year, having their young to protect.

I realized very often the startling sensation alone of a night at the helm, of having a painful stillness broken by these leviathans bursting the surface of the water with a noise like the roar of a great sea, uncomfortably near, reminding me of the Cape Frio adventure; and my crew, I am sure, were not less sensitive to the same feeling of an awful danger, however imaginary. One night in particular, dark and foggy I remember, Victor called me excitedly, saying that something dreadful ahead and drawing rapidly near had frightened him.

It proved to be a whale, for some reason that I could only guess at, threshing the sea with its huge body, and surging about in all directions, so that it puzzled me to know which way to steer to go clear. I thought at first, from the rumpus made, that a fight was going on, such

74

as we had once witnessed from the deck of the *Aquid-neck*, not far from this place. Our course was changed as soon as we could decide which way to avoid, if possible, all marine disturbers of the peace. We wished especially to keep away from infuriated swordfish, which I feared might be darting about, and be apt to give us a blind thrust. Knowing that they somctimes pierce stout ships through with their formidable weapons, I began to feel ticklish about the ribs myself, I confess, and the little watch below, too, got uneasy and sleepless; for one of these swords, they knew well, would reach through and through our little boat, from keel to deck. Large ships have occasionally been sent into port leaky from the stab of a sword, but what I most dreaded was the possibility of one of us being ourselves pinned in the boat.

A swordfish once pierced a whale-ship through the planking, and through the solid frame timber and the thick ceiling, with his sword, leaving it there, a valuable plug indeed, with the point, it was found upon unshipping her cargo at New Bedford, even piercing through a cask in the hold.

CHAPTER XII

Sail from Frio—Round Cape St. Thome—High seas and swift currents—In the "trades"—Dangerous reefs—Run into harbour unawares, on a dark and stormy night—At Caravellas—Fine weather—A gale—Port St. Paulo—Treacherous natives—Sail for Bahia.

JULY 30th, early in the day, and after a pleasant visit at the cape, we sailed for the north, securing first a few sea shells to be cherished, with the *Thetis* relics, in remembrance of a most enjoyable visit to the hospitable shores of Cape Frio.

Having now doubled Cape Frio, a prominent point in our voyage, and having had the seaworthiness of our little ship thoroughly tested, as already told; and seeing, moreover, that we had nothing to fear from common small fry of the sea (one of its greatest monsters having failed to capsize us), we stood on with greater confidence than ever, but watchful, nevertheless, for any strange event that might happen.

A fresh polar wind hurried us on, under shortened sail, toward the softer "trades" of the tropics, but, veering to the eastward by midnight, it brought us well in with the land. Then, "Larboard watch, ahoy! all hands on deck and turn out reefs," was the cry. To weather Cape St. Thome we must lug on all sail. And we go over the shoals with a boiling sea and current in our favour. In twenty-four hours from Cape Frio, we had lowered the Southern Cross three degrees—180 miles.

Sweeping by the cape, the canoe sometimes standing on end, and sometimes buried in the deep hollow of the sea, we sunk the light on St. Thome soon out of sight and stood on with flowing sheet. The wind on the fol-' lowing day settled into regular south-east "trades," and our cedar canoe skipped briskly along, over friendly seas that were leaping toward home, doffing their crests onward and forward, but never back, and the splashing waves against her sides, then rippling along the thin cedar planks between the crew and eternity, vibrated enchanting music to the ear, while confidence grew in the bark that was HOMEWARD BOUND.

But coming upon coral reefs, of a dark night, while we listened to the dismal tune of the seas breaking over them with an eternal roar, how intensely lonesome they were! no sign of any living thing in sight, except, perhaps, the phosphorescent streaks of a hungry shark, which told of bad company in our wake, and made the gloom of the place more dismal still.

One night we made shelter under the lee of the extensive reefs called the Paredes (walls), without seeing the breakers at all in the dark, although they were not far in the distance. At another time, dragging on sail to clear a lee shore, of a dark and stormy night, we came suddenly into smooth water, where we cast anchor and furled our sails, lying in a magic harbour till daylight the next morning, when we found ourselves among a maze of ugly reefs, with high seas breaking over them, as far as the eye could reach, on all sides, except at the small entrance to the place that we had stumbled into in the night. The position of this future harbour is South Lat. 16° 48′, and West Long. from Greenwich 39° 30′. We named the place "PORT LIBERDADE."

The next places sighted were the treacherous Abrohles, and the village of Caravellas back of the reef where, upon refitting, I found that a chicken cost a thousand reis, a bunch of bananas four hundred reis; but where a dozen limes cost only twenty reis—one cent. Much whaling gear lay strewn about the place, and on the beach was the carcass of a whale about nine days slain. Also leaning against a smart-looking boat was a grey-haired fisherman, boat and man relics of New Bedford, employed at this station in their familiar industry. The old man was bare-footed and thinly clad, after the custom in this climate. Still, I recognized the fisherman and sailor in the set and rig of the few duds he had on, and the ample straw hat (donkey's breakfast) that he wore, and doffed in a seaman-like manner, upon our first salute. *"Filio do Mar do Nord Americano,"* said an affable native close by, pointing at the same time to that "son of the sea of North America," by way of introduction, as soon as it was learned that we, too, were of that country. I tried to learn from this ancient mariner the cause of his being stranded in this strange land. He may have been cast up there by the whale for aught I could learn to the contrary.

Choosing a berth well to windward of the dead whale—the one that landed "the old man of the sea" there, maybe!—we anchored for the night, put a light in the rigging and turned in. Next morning, the village was astir betimes; canoes were being put afloat, and the rattle of poles, paddles, bait boxes, and many more things for the daily trip that were being hastily put into each canoe, echoed back from the tall palm groves notes of busy life, telling us that it was time to weigh anchor and be sailing. To this cheerful tune we lent ear and, hastening to be underweigh, were soon clear of the port. Then, skimming along near the beach in the early morning, our sails spread to a land breeze, laden with fragrance from the tropic forest and the music of many songsters, we sailed in great felicity, dreading no dangers

78

from the sea, for there were none now to dread or fear.

Proceeding forward through this belt of moderate winds, fanned by alternating land and sea breezes, we drew on toward a region of high trade-winds that reach sometimes the dignity of a gale. It was no surprise, therefore, after days of fine-weather sailing, to be met by a storm, which so happened as to drive us into the indifferent anchorage of St. Paulo, thirty miles from Bahia, where we remained two days for shelter.

Time, three days from Caravellas; distance sailed, 270 miles.

A few fishermen lounged about the place, living, apparently, in wretched poverty, spending their time between waiting for the tide to go out, when it was in, and waiting for it to come in, when it was out, to float a canoe or bring fish to their shiftless nets. This, indeed, seemed their only concern in life; while their ill-thatched houses, forsaken of the adobe that once clung to the wicker walls, stood grinning in rows, like emblems of our mortality.

We found at this St. Paulo anything but saints. The wretched place should be avoided by strangers, unless driven there for shelter, as we ourselves were, by stress of weather. We left the place on the first lull of the wind, having been threatened by an attack from à gang of rough, half-drunken fellows, who rudely came on board, jostling about, and jabbering in a dialect which, however, I happened to understand. I got rid of them by the use of my broken Portuguese, and once away I was resolved that they should stay away. I was not mistaken in my suspicions that they would return and try to come aboard, which shortly afterward they did, but my resolution to keep them off was not shaken. I let them know, in their own jargon this time, that I was well armed. They finally paddled back to the shore, and all visiting was then ended. We stood a good watch that night, and by daylight next morning, Aug. 12th, put to sea, standing out in a heavy swell, the character of which I knew better, and could trust to more confidently than a harbour among treacherous natives.

Early in the same day, we arrived at *Bahia do todos Santos* (All Saints' Bay), a charming port, with a rich surrounding country. It was from this port, by the way, that Robinson Crusoe sailed for Africa to procure slaves for his plantation and that of his friend, so fiction relates.

At Bahia we met many friends and gentle folk. Not the least interesting at this port are the negro lasses of fine physique seen at the markets and in the streets, with burdens on their heads of baskets of fruit, or jars of water, which they balance with ease and grace, as they go sweeping by with that stately mien which the dusky maiden can call her own.

CHAPTER XIII

At Bahia—Meditations on the discoverers—The Caribbees.

A T Bahia we refitted, with many necessary provisions, and repaired the keel, which we found, upon hauling out, had been damaged by the encounter with the whale at Frio. An iron shoe was now added for the benefit of all marine monsters wishing to scratch their backs on our canoe.

Among the many friends whom we met at Bahia were Capt. Boyd and his family of the bark *H. W. Palmer*. We shall meet the *Palmer* and the Boyds again on the voyage. They were old traders to South America and had many friends at this port who combined to make our visit a pleasant one. And their little son Rupert was greatly taken with the "*Rib*erdade," as he called her, coming often to see us. And the officials of the port taking great interest in our voyage, came often on board. No one could have treated us more kindly than they.

The venerable *Administradore* himself gave us special welcome to the port and a kind word upon our departure, accompanied by a present for my wife in the shape of a rare white flower, which we cherished greatly as coming from a true gentleman.

Some strong abolitionists at the port would have us dine in an epicurean way in commemoration of the name given our canoe, which was adopted because of her having been put afloat on the thirteenth day of May, the day on which every human being in Brazil could say, "I have no master but one." I declined the banquet tendered us, having work on hand, fortifying the canoe against the ravaging worms of the seas we were yet to sail through, bearing in mind the straits of my great predecessor from this as well as other causes on his voyage over the Caribbean Seas. I was bound to be strengthened against the enemy.

The gout, it will be remembered, seized upon the good Columbus while his ship had worms, when both ship and admiral lay stranded among menacing savages; surrounded, too, by a lawless, threatening band of his own countrymen not less treacherous than the worst of cannibals. His state was critical indeed! One calamity was from over-high living—this I was bound to guard against—the other was from neglect on the part of his people to care for the ship in a seaman-like manner. Of the latter difficulty I had no risk to run.

Lazy and lawless, but through the pretext of religion, the infected crew wrought on the pious feelings of the good admiral, inducing him at every landing to hold mass instead of cleaning the foul ship. Thus through petty intrigue and grave neglects, they brought disaster and sorrow on their leader and confusion on their own heads. Their religion, never deep, could not be expected to keep *Terredo* from the ship's bottom, so her timbers were ravished, and ruin came to them all! Poor Columbus! had he but sailed with his son Diego and his noble brother Bartholomew, for his only crew and companions, not forgetting the help of a good woman, America would have been discovered without those harrowing tales of woe and indeed heartrending calamities which followed in the wake of his designing people. Nor would his ship have been less well manned than was the *Liberdade*, sailing, centuries after, over the same sea and among many of the islands visited by the great discoverer—sailing, too, without serious accident of any kind, and without sickness or discontent. Our advantage

82

over Columbus, I say, was very great, not more from the possession of data of the centuries which had passed than from having a willing crew sailing without dissent or murmur—sailing in the same boat, as it were.

A pensive mood comes over one voyaging among the scenes of the New World's early play-ground. To us while on this canoe voyage of pleasant recollection the fancied experience of navigators gone before was intensely thrilling.

Sailing among islands clothed in eternal green, the same that Columbus beheld with marvellous anticipations, and the venerable Las Casas had looked upon with pious wonder, brought us, in the mind's eye, near the old discoverers; and a feeling that we should come suddenly upon their ships around some near headland took deep hold upon our thoughts as we drew in with the shores. All was there to please the imagination and dream over in the same balmy, sleepy atmosphere, where Juan Ponce de Leon would fain have tarried young, but found death rapid, working side by side with ever springing life. To live long in this clime one must obey great Nature's laws. So stout Juan and millions since have found, and so always it will be.

All was there to testify as of yore, all except the first owners of the land; they alas! the poor Caribbees, together with their camp fires, had been extinguished long years before. And no one of human sympathy can read of the cruel tortures and final extermination of these islanders, savages though they were, without a pang of regret at the unpleasant page in a history of glory and civilization.

CHAPTER XIV

Bahia to Pernambuco—The meeting of the *Finance* at sea—At
Pernambuco—Round Cape St. Roque—A gale—Breakers—
The stretch to Barbadoes—Flying-fish alighting on deck—
Dismasted—Arrive at Carlysle Bay.

FROM Bahia to Pernambuco our course lay along that
part of the Brazilian coast fanned by constant trade-
winds. Nothing unusual occurred to disturb our peace
or daily course, and we pressed forward night and day,
as was our wont from the first.

Victor and I stood watch and watch at sea, usually
four hours each.

The most difficult of our experiences in fine weather
was the intense drowsiness brought on by constantly
watching the oscillating compass at night: even in the
daytime this motion would make one sleepy.

We soon found it necessary to arrange a code of signals which would communicate between the tiller and
the "man forward." This was accomplished by means
of a line or messenger extending from one to the other,
which was understood by the number of pulls given by
it; three pulls, for instance, meant "Turn out," one in
response, "Aye, aye, I am awake, and what is it that is
wanted?" one pull in return signified that it was
"Eight bells," and so on. But three quick jerks meant
"Tumble out and shorten sail."

Victor, it was understood, would tie the line to his
arm or leg when he turned in, so that by pulling I
would be sure to arouse him, or bring him somewhat
unceremoniously out of his bunk. Once, however, the
messenger failed to accomplish its purpose. A boot came

out on the line in answer to my call, so easily, too, that I suspected a trick. It was evidently a preconceived plan by which to gain a moment more of sleep. It was a clear imposition on the man at the wheel!

We had also a sign in this system of telegraphing that told of flying-fish on board—manna of the sea—to be gathered up for the *cuisine* whenever they happened to alight or fall on deck, which was often, and as often they found a warm welcome.

The watch was never called to make sail. As for myself, I had never to be called, having thoughts of the voyage and its safe completion on my mind to keep me always on the alert. I can truly say that I never, on the voyage, slept so sound as to forget where I was, but whenever I fell into a doze at all it would be to dream of the boat and the voyage.

Press on! press on! was the watchword while at sea, but in port we enjoyed ourselves and gave up care for rest and pleasure, carrying a supply, as it were, to sea with us, where sail was again carried on.

Though a mast should break, it would be no matter of serious concern, for we would be at no loss to mend and rig up spars for this craft at short notice, most anywhere.

The third day out from Bahia was set fine weather. A few flying-fish made fruitless attempts to rise from the surface of the sea, attracting but little attention from the sea-gulls which sat looking wistfully across the unbroken deep with folded wings.

And the *Liberdade*, doing her utmost to get along through the common quiet, made but little progress on her way. A dainty fish played in her light wake, till tempted by an evil appetite for flies, it landed in the cockpit upon a hook, thence into the pan, where many a one had brought up before. Breakfast was cleared away

at an early hour; then day of good things happened—
"the meeting of the ships."

> When o'er the silent sea alone
>   For days and nights we've cheerless gone,
> Oh they who've felt it know how sweet,
>   Some sunny morn a sail to meet.
>
> Sparkling at once is every eye,
>   "Ship ahoy! ship ahoy!" our joyful cry
> While answering back the sound we hear,
>   "Ship ahoy! ship ahoy! what cheer, what cheer."
>
> Then sails are backed, we nearer come,
>   Kind words are said of friends and home,
> And soon, too soon, we part with pain,
>   To sail o'er silent seas again.

On the clear horizon could be seen a ship, which proved to be our staunch old friend, the *Finance*, on her way out to Brazil, heading nearly for us. Our course was at once changed, so as to cross her bows. She rose rapidly, hull up, showing her lines of unmistakable beauty, the Stars and Stripes waving over all. They on board the great ship soon descried our little boat, and gave sign by a deep whistle that came rumbling over the sea, telling us that we were recognized. A few moments later and the engines stopped. Then came the hearty hail, "Do you want assistance?" Our answer "No" brought cheer on cheer from the steamer's deck, while the *Liberdade* bowed and courtesied to her old acquaintance, the superior ship. Captain Baker, meanwhile, not forgetting a sailor's most highly prized luxury, had ordered in the slings a barrel of potatoes— new from home! Then dump they came, in a jiffy, into the canoe, giving her a settle in the water of some inches. Other fresh provisions were handed us, also some books and late papers. J. Aspinwill Hodge, D.D., on a tour of inspection in the interest of the Presbyterian Mission in Brazil—on deck here with his camera—got an excellent photograph of the canoe.[1]

One gentleman passed us a bottle of wine, on the label of which was written the name of an old acquaintance, a merchant of Rio. We pledged Mr. Gudgeon and all his fellow passengers in that wine, and had some left long after, to the health of the captain of the ship, and his crew. There was but little time for words, so the compliments passed were brief. The ample plates in the sides of the *Finance*, inspiring confidence in American thoroughness and build, we had hardly time to scan, when her shrill whistle said "good-bye," and moving proudly on, the great ship was soon out of sight, while the little boat, filling away on the starboard tack, sailed on toward home, perfumed with the interchange of a friendly greeting, tinged though with a palpable lonesomeness. Two days after this pleasant meeting, the Port of Pernambuco was reached.

Tumbling in before a fresh "trade" wind that in the evening had sprung up, accompanied with long, rolling seas, our canoe came nicely round the point between lighted reef and painted buoy.

Spray from the breakers on the reef opportunely wetting her sails gave them a flat surface to the wind as we came close haul.

The channel leading up the harbour was not strange to us, so we sailed confidently along the lee of the wonderful wall made by worms, to which alone Pernam-

---

[1] We had the pleasure of meeting this gentleman again on the voyage at Barbadoes, again at New London, and finally with delight we heard him lecture on his travels, at Newport, and saw there produced on the wall the very picture of the *Liberdade* taken by the doctor on the great ocean.

buco is indebted for its excellent harbour; which, extending also along a great stretch of the coast, protects Brazil from the encroachment of the sea.

At 8 p.m. we came to in a snug berth near the *Alfandega*, and early next morning received the official visit from the polite port officers.

Time from Bahia, five days; distance sailed, 390 miles.

Pernambuco, the principal town of a large and wealthy province of the same name, is a thriving place, sending out valuable cargoes, principally of sugar and cotton. I had loaded costly cargoes here, times gone by. I met my old merchant again this time, but could not carry his goods on the *Liberdade*. However, fruits from his orchards and a run among the trees refreshed my crew, and prepared them for the coming voyage to Barbadoes, which was made with expedition.

From Pernambuco we experienced a strong current in our favour, with, sometimes, a confused cross sea that washed over us considerably. But the swift current sweeping along through it all made compensation for discomforts of motion, though our "ups and downs" were many. Along this part of the coast (from Pernambuco to the Amazon), if one day should be fine, three stormy ones would follow, but the gale was always fair, carrying us forward at a goodly rate.

Along about half way from Cape St. Roque to the Amazon, the wind which had been blowing hard for two days, from E.S.E., and raising lively waves all about, increased to a gale that knocked up seas, washing over the little craft more than ever. The thing was becoming monotonous and tiresome; for a change, therefore, I ran in toward the land, so as to avoid the ugly cross sea farther out in the current. This course was a mistaken one; we had not sailed far on it when a sudden rise of the canoe, followed by an unusually long run down on the slope of a roller, told us of a danger that we hardly dared to think of, then a mighty comber broke, but, as Providence willed, broke short of the canoe, which under shortened sail was then scudding very fast.

We were on a shoal, and the sea was breaking from the bottom! The second great roller came on, towering up, up, up, until nothing longer could support the mountain of water, and it seemed only to pause before its fall to take aim and surely gather us up in its sweeping fury.

I put the helm a-lee; there was nothing else to do but this, and say prayers. The helm hard down, brought the canoe round, bows to the danger, while in breathless anxiety we prepared to meet the result as best we could. Before we could say "Save us, or we perish," the sea broke over with terrific force and passed on, leaving us trembling in His hand, more palpably helpless than ever before. Other great waves came madly on, leaping toward destruction; how they bellowed over the shoal! I could smell the slimy bottom of the sea, when they broke! I could tast the salty sand!

In this perilous situation, buried sometimes in the foaming breakers, and at times tossed like a reed on the crest of the waves, we struggled with might and main at the helm and the sheets, easing her up or forcing her ahead with care, gaining little by little toward deep water, till at last she came out of the danger, shook her feathers like a sea-bird, and rode on waves less perilous. Then we had time and courage to look back, but not till then.

And what a sight we beheld! The horizon was illumined with phosphorescent light from the breakers just passed through. The rainstorm which had obscured the coast was so cleared away now that we could see the whole field of danger behind us. One spot in particular, the place where the breakers dashed over a rock which appeared awash, in the glare flashed up a shaft of light that reached to the heavens.

This was the greatest danger we had yet encountered. The elasticity of our canoe, not its bulk, saved it from destruction. Her light, springy timbers and buoyant bamboo guards brought her upright again and again through the fierce breakers. We were astonished at the feats of wonder of our brave little craft.

Fatigued and worn with anxiety, when clear of the shoal we hauled to under close reefs, heading off shore, and all hands lay down to rest till daylight. Then, squaring away again, we set what sail the canoe could carry, scudding before it, for the wind was still in our favour, though blowing very hard. Nevertheless the weather seemed fine and pleasant at this stage of our own pleased feelings. Any weather that one's craft can live in, after escaping a lee shore, is pleasant weather—though some may be pleasanter than other.

What we most wished for, after this thrilling experience, was sea room, fair wind, and plenty of it. That these without stint would suit us best, was agreed on all hands. Accordingly then I shaped the course seaward, clearing well all the dangers of the land.

The fierce tropical storm of the last few days turned gradually into mild trade-winds, and our cedar canoe skipped nimbly once more over tranquil seas. Our own agitation, too, had gone down and we sailed on un-ruffled by care. Gentle winds carried us on over kindly waves, and we were fain to count fair days ahead, leaving all thoughts of stormy ones behind. In this hope-ful mood we sailed for many days, our spirits never lowering, but often rising higher out of the miserable condition which we had fallen into through misfortunes on the foreign shore. When a star came out, it came as a friend, and one that had been seen by friends of old. When all the stars shone out, the hour at sea was cheerful, bright, and joyous. Welby saw, or had in the mind's-eye, a day like many that we experienced in the soft, clear "trades" on this voyage, when writing the pretty lines:—

> The twilight hours like birds flew by,
>   As lightly and as free,
> Ten thousand stars were in the sky,
>   Ten thousand on the sea.
>
> For every rippling, dancing wave,
>   That leaped upon the air,
> Had caught a star in its embrace,
>   And held it trembling there.

"The days pass, and our ship flies fast upon her way."

For several days while sailing near the line we saw the constellations of both hemispheres, but heading north, we left those of the south at last, with the Southern Cross—most beautiful in all the heavens—to watch over a friend.

Leaving these familiar southern stars and sailing toward constellations in the north, we hoist all sail to the cheery breeze which carries us on.

In this pleasant state of sailing with our friends all about us, we stood on and on, never doubting once our pilot or our ship.

A phantom of the stately *Aquidneck* appeared one night, sweeping by with crowning skysails set, that fairly brushed the stars. No apparition could have affected us more than the sight of this floating beauty, so like the *Aquidneck*, gliding swiftly and quietly by, from her mission to some foreign land—she, too, was homeward bound!

This incident of the *Aquidneck's* ghost, as it appeared to us, passing at midnight on the sea, left a pang of lonesomeness for a while.

But a carrier dove came next day, and perched upon the mast, as if to tell that we had yet a friend! Welcome harbinger of good! you bring us thoughts of angels.

The lovely visitor remained with us two days, off and on, but left for good on the third, when we reached away from Avis Island, to which, maybe, it was bound. Coming as it did from the east, and flying west toward the island when it left, bore out the idea of the lay of sweet singer Kingsley's "Last Buccaneer."

> If I might but be a sea dove, I'd fly across the main
> To the pleasant Isle of Avis, to look at it once again.

The old Buccaneer, it may have been, but we regarded it as the little bird, which most likely it was, that sits up aloft to look out for poor "Jack." [1]

A moth, blown to our boat on the ocean, found shelter and a welcome there. The dove we secretly worshipped.

With utmost confidence in our little craft, inspired by many thrilling events, we now carried sail, blow high, blow low, till at times she reeled along with a bone in her mouth quite to the mind of her mariners. Thinking one day that she might carry more sail on the mast already bending hopefully forward, and acting upon the liberal thought of sail, we made a wide mistake, for the mainmast went by the board, under the extra press and the foremast tripped over the bows. Then spars, booms, and sails swung alongside like the broken wings

[1] There's a sweet little cherub that sits up aloft,
To look out for a berth for poor Jack.—*Dibdin's Poems.*

of a bird, but were grappled, however, and brought aboard without much loss of time. The broken mast was then secured and strengthened by "fishes" or splints after the manner in which doctors fish a broken limb.

Both of the masts were very soon refitted and again made to carry sail, all they could stand; and we were again bowling along as before. We made that day a hundred and seventy-five miles, one of our best days' work.

I protest here that my wife should not have cried "More sail! more sail!" when as it has been seen the canoe had on all the sail that she could carry. Nothing further happened to change the usual daily events until we reached Barbadoes. Flying-fish on the wing striking our sails, at night, often fell on deck, affording us many a toothsome fry. This happened daily, while sailing throughout the trade-wind regions. To be hit by one of these fish on the wing, which sometimes occurs, is no light matter, especially if the blow be on the face, as it may cause a bad bruise or even a black eye. The head of the flying-fish being rather hard makes it in fact a night slugger to be dreaded. They never come aboard in the daylight. The swift darting bill-fish, too, is a danger to be avoided in the tropics at night. They are met with mostly in the Pacific Ocean; therefore South Sea Islanders are loath to voyage during the "bill-fish season."

As to the flight of these fishes, I would estimate that of the flying-fish as not exceeding fifteen feet in height, or five hundred yards of distance, often not half so much.

Bill-fish, darting like an arrow from a bow, have, fortunately for sailors, not the power or do not rise much above the level of the waves, and cannot dart further, say, than two hundred and fifty feet, according to the day for jumping. Of the many swift fish in the sea, the dolphin, perhaps, is the most marvellous. Its oft-told beauty, too, is indeed remarkable. A few of these fleet racers were captured, on the voyage, but were found tough and rank; notwithstanding some eulogy on them by other epicures, we threw the mess away. Those hooked by my crew were perhaps the tyrrhena pirates "turned into dolphins" in the days of yore.

On the 19th day from Pernambuco, early in the morning, we made Barbadoes away in the West. First, the blue, fertile hills, then green fields came into view, studded with many white buildings between sentries of giant wind-mills as old nearly as the hills. Barbadoes is the most pleasant island in the Antilles; to sail round its green fringe of coral sea is simply charming. We stood in to the coast, well to windward, sailing close in with the breakers so as to take in a view of the whole delightful panorama as we sailed along. By noon we rounded the south point of the island and shot into Carlysle Bay, completing the run from Pernambuco exactly in nineteen days. This was considerably more than an hundred miles a day. The true distance being augmented by the circuitous route we adopted made it 2,150 miles.

CHAPTER XV

At Barbadoes—Mayaguez—Crossing the Bahama Banks—The Gulf Stream—Arrival on the coast of South Carolina.

MANY old friends and acquaintances came down to see us upon our arrival at Barbadoes, all curious to inspect the strange craft. While there our old friend, the *Palmer*, that we left at Bahia, came in to refit, having broken a mast "trying to beat us," so Garfield would have it. For all that we had beaten her by four days. Who then shall say that we anchored nights or spent much time hugging the shore? The *Condor* was also at Barbadoes in charge of an old friend, accompanied by a pleasant helpmeet and companion who had shared the perils of shipwreck with her husband the year before in a hurricane among the islands.

Meeting so many of this class of old friends of vast and varied experiences gave contentment to our visit, and we concluded to remain over at this port till the hurricane season should pass. Our old friend, the *Finance*, too, came in, remaining but a few hours. However, she hurried away with her mails, homeward bound.

The pleasant days at Barbadoes with its enchantment flew lightly by; and on the 7th of October we sailed, giving the hurricane season the benefit of eight days. The season is considered over on the 15th of that month.

Passing thence through the Antilles into the Caribbean Sea, a new period of our voyage was begun. Fair breezes filled the sails of the *Liberdade* as we glided along over tranquil seas, scanning eagerly the islands as they

95

came into view, dwelling on each, in our thoughts, as hallowed ground of the illustrious discoverers—the same now as seen by them! The birds, too, of "rare plumage," were there, flying from island to island, the same as seen by the discoverers; and the sea with fishes teemed, of every gorgeous hue, lending enchantment to the picture, not less beautiful than the splendour on the land and in the air to thrill the voyager now, the same as then; we ourselves had only to look to see them.

Whether it was birds with fins, or fishes with wings, or neither of these that the old voyagers saw, they discovered yet enough to make them wonder and rejoice.

"Mountains of sugar, and rivers of rum and flying-fish, was what I saw, mother," said the son on his return from a voyage to these islands. "John," said the enraptured mother, "you must be mistaken about the fish; now don't lie to me, John. Mountains of sugar, no doubt you saw, and even rivers of rum, my boy, but *flying-fish* could never be."

And yet the *fish* were there.

Among the islands of great interest which came in view, stretching along the Caribbean Sea, was that of Santa Cruz, the island famous for its brave, resolute women of days gone by, who, while their husbands were away, successfully defended home and happiness against Christian invaders, and for that reason were called fierce savages. I would fain have brought away some of the earth of the island in memory of those brave women. Small as our ship was, we could have afforded room in it for a memento thus consecrated; but the trades hauling somewhat to the northward so headed us off that we had to forgo the pleasure of landing on its shores.

Pushing forward thence, we reached Porto Rico, the nearest land in our course from the Island of Brave

AN ODD PHOTOGRAPH

Women, standing well in with the southeast capes. Sailing thence along the whole extent of the south coast, in waters as smooth as any mill pond, and past island scenery worth the perils of ten voyages to see, we landed, on the 12th of October, at Mayaguez in the west of the island, and there shook the kinks out of our bones by pleasant walks in tropic shades.

Time, five days from Barbadoes; distance 570 miles.

This was to be our last run among the trees in the West Indies, and we made the most of it. "Such a port for mariners I'll never see again!" The port officials, kind and polite, extended all becoming courtesies to the quaint *"barco piquina."*

The American Consul, Mr. Christie, Danish Consul, Mr. Falby, and the good French Consul, vied in making our visit a pleasant one.

Photographers at Mayaguez desiring a picture of the canoe with the crew on deck at a time when we felt inclined to rest in the shade on shore, put a negro on board to take the place of captain. The photographs taken then found their way to Paris and Madrid journals where, along with some flattering accounts, they were published, upon which it was remarked that the captain was a fine-looking fellow, but "awfully tanned!" The moke was rigged all ataunto for the occasion, and made a picture indicative of great physical strength, one not to be ashamed of, but he would have looked more like me, I must say, if they had turned him back to.

We enjoyed long carriage drives over rich estates at Mayaguez. We saw with pain, however, that the atmosphere of the soldier hung over all, pervading the whole air like a pestilence.

Musketed and sabred and uniformed in their bed-ticking suits; hated by the residents and despised by

97

themselves, they doggedly marched, counter-marched and wheeled, knowing that they are loathsome in the island, and that their days in the New World are numbered. The sons of the colonies are too civil and Christianlike to be ruled always by sword and gun.

On the 15th of October, after three days' rest, we took in, as usual before sailing from ports, sufficient fresh supplies to carry us to the port steered for next, then set sail from pleasant Mayaguez, and bore away for the old Bahama Channel, passing east of Hayti, thence along the north coast to the west extremity of the island, from which we took departure for the headlands of Cuba, and followed that coast as far as Cardinas, where we took a final departure from the islands, regretting that we could not sail around them all.

The region on the north side of Cuba is often visited by gales of great violence, making this the lee shore; a weather eye was therefore kept lifting, especially in the direction of their source, which is from north to nor'-west. However, storms prevailed from other quarters, mostly from the east, bringing heavy squalls of wind, rain and thunder every afternoon, such as once heard will never be forgotten. Peal on peal of nature's artillery for a few hours, accompanied by vivid lightning, was on the cards for each day, then all would be serene again.

The nights following these severe storms were always bright and pleasant, and the heavens would be studded with constellations of familiar, guiding stars.

My crew had now no wish to bear up for port short of one on our own coast, but, impatient to see the North Star appear higher in the heavens, strung every nerve and trimmed every sail to hasten on.

Nassau, the place to which letters had been directed to us, we forbore to visit. This departure from a programme which was made at the beginning was the only

98

change that we made in the "charter party" throughout the voyage. There was no haphazard sailing on this voyage. Daily observations for determining latitude and longitude were invariably made unless the sun was obscured. The result of these astronomical observations were more reliable than one might suppose, from their being taken on a tittlish canoe. After a few days' practising, a very fair off-hand contact could be made, when the canoe rose on the crest of a wave, where manifestly would be found the best result. The observer's station was simply on the top of the cabin, where astride, like riding horseback, Victor and I took the "sights," and indeed became expert "snap observers" before the voyage ended.

One night in the Bahama Channel, while booming along toward the Banks to the nor'west of us before stiff trades, I was called in the first watch by Victor, to come up quickly, for signs of the dread "norther" were in the sky. Our trusty barometer had been low, but was now on the cheerful side of change. This phenomenon disturbed me somewhat, till the discovery was made, as we came nearer, that it was but the reflection of the white banks on the sky that we saw, and no cause at all for alarm.

Soon after this phenomenon the faint glimmer of Lobos Light was descried flickering on the horizon, two points on the weather bow. I changed the course three points to windward, having determined to touch at the small Cay where the lighthouse stands; one point being allowed for leeway, which I found was not too much.

Three hours later we fetched in under the lee of the reef, or Cay, as it is commonly called, and came to in one and a half fathoms of water in good shelter.

We beheld then overhead in wonderful beauty what had awed us from the distance in the early night—a chart of the illuminating banks marked visibly on the heavens.

We furled sails and, setting a light in the rigging, turned in; for it lacked three hours yet of daylight. And what an interesting experience ours had been in the one short night! By the break of day my crew were again astir, preparing to land and fill water at a good landing which we now perceived farther around the point to leeward, where the surf was moderate.

On the Cay is stored some hundred thousand gallons of rain water in cisterns at the base of the iron tower which carries the light; one that we saw from the canoe at a distance of fourteen miles.

The keeper of the light, a hardy native of Nassau, when he discovered the new arrival at his "island," hoisted the British Board of Trade flag on a pole in the centre of this, his little world, then he came forward to speak us, thinking at first, he said, that we were ship-wrecked sailors, which indeed we were, but not in dis-tress, as he had supposed when hoisting the flag, which signified assistance for distressed seamen. On learning our story, however, he regarded us with grave sus-picions, and refused water to Victor, who had already landed with buckets, telling him that the captain would have to bring his papers ashore and report. The mate's report would not be taken. Thus in a moment was transformed the friend in need to *governor of an island.* This amused me greatly, and I sent back word to my veritable Sancho Panza that in my many voyages to islands my mate had attended to the customs reports; at which his Excellency chafed considerably, giving the gunnels of his trousers a fitful tug up now and then as he paced the beach, waiting my compliance with the rules of the island. The governor, I perceived, was sus-picious of smugglers and wreckers, apparently understanding their ways, if, indeed, even he were not a reformed pirate himself.

However, to humour the punctiliousness of his Excellency, now that he was governor of an island, I placed my papers in my hat, and, leaping into the surf, waded ashore, where I was received as by a monarch.

The document I presented was the original *Passe Especial*, the one with the big seal on it, written in Portuguese; had it been in Choctàw the governor would have read it with the same facility that he did this, which he stared at knowingly and said, "all right, take all the water you want; it is free."

I lodged a careful report of the voyage with the governor and explained to his Excellency the whereabouts of the "Island of Rio," as his grace persistently called Rio de Janeiro, whence dated my papers.

Conversing on the subject of islands, which was all the world to him, the governor viewed with suspicion the absence of a word in my documents, referring even to an islet; this, in his mind, was a reprehensible omission; for surely New York, to which the papers referred, was built on an island. Upon this I offered to swear to the truth of my clearance, "as far as known to me," after the manner of cheap custom-house swearing with which shipmasters, in some parts of the world, are made familiar. "Not on the island!" quickly exclaimed the governor, " 'for thou shalt not disglorify God's name,' is written in the Bible."

I assured the governor of my appreciation of his pious sentiment of not over-swearing,—a laudable plan that even the Chinese adopt as a policy, and one that I would speak of on my return home, to the end that we all emulate the laws of the island; whereupon the governor, greatly pleased, urged me to take some more water, minding me again that it was free.

In a very few minutes I got all the water I wished for; also some aurora shells from the governor's lady, who had arisen with the sun to grace the day and of all things most appropriate held in her generous lap beautiful aurora shells for which—to spoil the poem—I bartered cocoa-nuts and rusty gnarly yams.

The lady was on a visit only to her lord and master, the monarch of all he surveyed. Beside this was their three children also on a visit, from Nassau, and two assistant keepers of the light which made up the total of this little world in the ocean.

It was the smallest kingdom I had ever visited, peopled by happy human beings and the most isolated by far.

The few blades of grass which had struggled into existence, not enough to support a goat, was all there was to look at on the island except the lighthouse, and the sand and themselves.

Some small buildings and a flagstaff had once adorned the place, but together with a coop of chickens, the only stock of the islanders—except a dog—had been swept away by a hurricane which had passed over the island a short time before. The water for which we had called being now in the canoe, and my people on board waiting for me, I bade the worthy governor good-bye, and, saluting his charming island queen in a seamanlike manner, hastened back to my own little world; and bore away once more for the north. Sailing thence over the Great Bahama Banks, in a crystal sea, we observed on the white marl bottom many curious living things, among them the conch in its house of exquisite tints and polished surface, the star-fish with radiated dome of curious construction, and many more denizens of the place, the names of which I could not tell, resting on the soft white bed under the sea.

"They who go down to the sea in ships, they see the wonders of the Lord," I am reminded by a friend who writes me, on receipt of some of these curious things which I secured on the voyage, adding: "For all these curious and beautiful things are His handiwork. Who can look at such things without the heart being lifted up in adoration?"

For words like these what sailor is there who would not search the caves of the ocean? Words too, from a lady.

Two days of brisk sailing over the white Bahama Banks brought us to Bimini. Thence a mere push would send us to the coast of our own native America. The wind in the meantime hauling from regular nor'-east trade to the sou'west, as we came up to Bimini, promising a smooth passage across, we launched out at once on the great Gulf Stream, and were swept along by its restless motion, making on the first day, before the wind and current, two hundred and twenty miles. This was great getting along for a small canoe. Going at the same high rate of speed on the second night in the stream, the canoe struck a spar and went over it with a bound. Her keel was shattered by the shock, but finally shaking the crippled timber clear of herself she came on quite well without it. No other damage was done to our craft, although at times her very ribs were threatened before clearing this lively ocean river. In the middle of the current, where the seas were yet mountainous but regular, we went along with a wide, swinging motion and fared well enough; but on nearing the edge of the stream a confused sea was met with, standing all on end, in every which way, beyond a sailor's comprehension. The motion of the *Liberdade* was then far from poetical or pleasant. The wind, in the meantime, had chopped round to the nor'east, dead ahead; being thus against the current, a higher and more confused sea than ever was heaped up, giving us some uneasiness. We had, indeed, several unwelcome visitors come tumbling aboard of our craft, one of which furiously crashing down on her made all of her timbers bend and creak. However, I could partially remedy this danger by changing the course.

"Seas like that can't break this boat," said our young boatswain; "she's built strong." It was well to find among the crew this feeling of assurance in the gallant little vessel. I, too, was confident in her seaworthiness. Nevertheless, I shortened sail and brought her to the wind, watching the lulls and easing her over the combers, as well as I could. But wrathful Neptune was not to let us so easily off, for the next moment a sea swept clean over the helmsman, wetting him through to the skin and, most unkind cut of all, it put out our fire, and capsized the hash and stove into the bottom of the canoe. This left us with but a *damper* for breakfast! Matters mended, however, as the day advanced, and for supper we had a grand and glorious feast. Early in the afternoon we made the land and got into smooth water. This of itself was a feast, to our minds.

The land we now saw lying before us was hills of America, which we had sailed many thousands of miles to see. Drawing in with the coast, we made out, first the broad, rich forests, then open fields and villages, with many signs of comfort on every hand. We found it was the land about Bull's Bay on the coast of South Carolina, and night coming on, we could plainly see Cape Roman Light to the north of us. The wind falling light as we drew in with the coast, and finding a current against us, we anchored, about two miles from the shore, in four fathoms of water. It was now 8 p.m., October 28,

1888, thirteen days from Mayaguez, twenty-one days from Barbadoes, etc.

The following was the actual time at sea and distances in nautical miles from point to point on the courses steered, approximately:

		Days.	Distance.
From Paranagua to Santos		1	150
„ Santos to Rio de Janeiro (towed by *Finance*) . . .		¾	200
„ Rio to Cape Frio		2	70
„ Cape Frio to Carvellas . . .		4	370
„ Carvellas to Saint Paulo . . .		3	270
„ Saint Paulo to Bahia		½	40
„ Bahia to Pernambuco. . . .		5	390
„ Pernambuco to Barbadoes . . .		19	2,150
„ Barbadoes to Mayaguez . . .		5	570
„ Mayaguez to Cape Roman . . .		13	1,300
		53¼	5,510

Computing all the distances of the ins and outs that we made would considerably augment the sum. To say, therefore, that the *Liberdade* averaged a hundred and three miles a day for fifty-three days would be considerably inside the truth.

This was the voyage made in the boat which cost less than a hundred dollars outside of our own labour of building. Journals the world over have spoken not unkindly of the feat; encomiums in seven languages reached us through the newspapers while we lay moored in Washington. Should the same good fortune that followed the *Liberdade* attend this little literary craft, when finished, it would go safe into many lands. Without looking, however, to this mark of good fortune, the journal of the voyage has been as carefully constructed as was the *Liberdade*, and I trust, as conscientiously, by a hand, alas! that has grasped the sextant more often than the plane or pen, and for the love of doing. This apology might have been more appropriately made in the beginning of the journal, maybe, but it comes to me now, and like many other things done, right or wrong, but done on the impulse of the moment, I put it down.

CHAPTER XVI

Ocean Currents—Visit to South Santee—At the Typee River—
Quarantined—South Port and Wilmington, N.C.—Inland
sailing to Beaufort, Norfolk and Washington, D.C.—
Voyage ended.

NO one will be more surprised at the complete success
of the voyage and the speedy progress made than
were we ourselves who made it.

A factor of the voyage, one that helped us forward
greatly, and which is worthy of special mention, was
the ocean current spoken of as we came along in its
friendly sway,

Many are the theories among fresh water philoso-
phists respecting these currents, but in practical sailing,
where the subject is met with in its tangible form, one
cause only is recognized; namely, the action of the wind
on the surface of the water, pushing the waves along.
Out on the broad ocean the effect at first is hardly per-
ceptible, but the constant trades, sending countless millions of waves in one direction, cause at last a mighty
moving power, which the mariner meets sometimes as
an enemy to retard and delay, sometimes as a friend, as
in our case, to help him on his way. These are views
from a practical experience with no theory to prove.

By daylight on the twenty-ninth, we weighed anchor
and set sail again for the north. The wind and current
were still adverse, but we kept near the land, making
short boards off and on through the day where the current had least effect. And when night came on again
we closed in once more with Cape Roman light.
Next day we worked up under the lee of the Roman

shoals and made harbour in South Santee, a small river to the north ot Cape Roman, within range of the light, there to rest until the wind should change, it being still ahead.

Next morning, since the wind had not changed, we weighed anchor and stood farther into the river looking for inhabitants, that we might listen to voices other than our own. Our search was soon rewarded, for, coming around a point of woodland, a farmhouse stood before us on the river side. We came alongside the bank and jumped ashore, but hardly had we landed when, as out of the earth, a thousand dogs, so it seemed, sprung up threatening to devour us all. However, a comely woman came out of the house and it was explained to the satisfaction of all, especially to a persistent cur, by a vigorous whack on the head with a cudgel, that our visit was a friendly one; then all was again peaceful and quiet. The good man was in the field close by, but soon came home accompanied by his two stalwart sons each "toting" a sack of corn. We found the Andersons—this was the family name—isolated in every sense of the word, and as primitive as heart could wish. The charming simplicity of these good people captivated my crew. We met others along the coast innocent of greed, but of all unselfish men, Anderson the elder was surely the prince.

Purchasing some truck from this good man, we found that change could not be made for the dollar which I tendered in payment. But I protested that I was more than content to let the few odd cents go, having received more garden stuff than I had ever seen offered for a dollar in any part of the world. And indeed I was satisfied. The farmer, however, nothing content, offered me a coon skin or two, but these I didn't want, and there being no other small change about the farm, the matter was dropped, I thought, for good, and I had quite forgotten it, when later in the evening I was electrified by his offering to carry a letter for us which we wished posted, some seven miles away, and call it "square," against the twenty cents of the morning's transaction. The letter went, and in due course of time we got an answer.

I do not say that we stuck strictly to the twenty-cent transaction, but I fear that not enough was paid to fair-dealing Anderson. However, all were at last satisfied and warming into conversation, a log fire was improvised and social chat went round.

These good people could hardly understand how it was, as I explained, that the Brazilians had freed the slaves and had no war, Mr. Anderson often exclaiming, "Well, well, I d'clar. Freed the niggers, and had no wah. Mister," said he, turning to me after a long pause, "mister, d'ye know the South were foolish? They had a wah, and they had to free the niggers, too."

"Oh, yes, mister, I was thar! Over thar beyond them oaks was my house."

"Yes, mister, I fought, too, and fought hard, but it warn't no use."

Like many a hard fighter, Anderson, too, was a pious man, living in a state of resignation to be envied. His years of experience on the new island farm had been hard and trying in the extreme. My own misfortunes passed into shade as the harder luck of the Andersons came before my mind, and the resolution which I had made to buy a farm was now shaken and finally dissolved into doubts of the wisdom of such a course. On this farm they had first "started in to raise pork," but found that it "didn't pay, for the pigs got wild and had to be gathered with the dogs," and by the time they were "gathered and then toted, salt would hardly cure them, and they most generally tainted." The enterprise was therefore abandoned, for that of tilling the soil, and a crop was put in, but "the few pigs which the dogs had not gathered came in at night and rooted out all the taters." It then appeared that a fence should be built. "Accordingly," said he, "the boys and I made one which kept out the stock, but, sir, the rats could get in! They took every tater out of the ground! From all that I put in, and my principal work was thar, I didn't see a sprout." How it happened that the rats had left the crop the year before for their relations—the pigs—was what seemed most to bother the farmer's mind. Nevertheless, "there was corn in Egypt yet"; and at the family circle about the board that night a smile of hope played on the good farmer's face, as in deep sincerity he asked that for what they had they might be made truly thankful. We learned a lesson of patience from this family, and were glad that the wind had carried us to their shore.

Said the farmer, "And you came all the way from Brazil in that boat! Wife, she won't go to Georgetown in the batto that I built because it rares too much. And they freed the niggers and had no wah! Well, well, I d'clar!"

Better folks we may never see than the farmers of South Santee. Bidding them good-bye next morning at early dawn we sailed before a light land wind which, however, soon petered out.

The S.S. *Planter* then coming along took us in tow for Georgetown, where she was bound. We had not the pleasure, however, of visiting the beloved old city; for having some half dozen cocoa-nuts on board, the remainder of small stores of the voyage, a vigilant officer stopped us at the quarantine ground. Fruit not being admitted into South Carolina until after the first of

November, and although it was now late in the afternoon of the first, we had to ride quarantine that night, with a promise, however, of *pratique* next morning. But there was no steamer going up the river the next day. The *Planter* coming down though supplied us with some small provisions, such as were not procurable at the Santee farm. Then putting to sea we beat along slowly against wind and current.

We began now to experience, as might be expected, autumn gales of considerable violence, the heaviest of which overtaking us at Frying-pan Shoal, drove us back to leeward of Cape Fear for shelter. South Port and Wilmington being then so near we determined to visit both places. Two weeks at these ports refreshed the crew and made all hands willing for sea again.

Sailing thence through Corn-cake Inlet we cut off Cape Fear and the Frying-pan Shoals, being of mind to make for the inlets along the Carolina coast and to get into the inland waters as soon as practicable.

It was our good fortune to fall in with an old and able pilot at Corn-cake Inlet, one Capt. Bloodgood, who led the way through the channel in his schooner, the *Packet*, a Carolina pitch and cotton droger of forty tons register, which was manned solely by the captain and his two sons, one twelve and the other ten years old. It was in the crew that I became most interested, and not the schooner. Bloodgood gave the order when the tide served for us to put to sea. "Come, children," said he, "let's try it." Then we all tried it together, the *Packet* leading the way. The shaky west wind, that filled our sails as we skimmed along the beach with the breakers close aboard, carried us but a few leagues when it flew suddenly round to nor'east and began to pipe.

The gale increasing rapidly inclined me to bear up for New River Inlet, then close under our lee, with a treacherous bar lying in front, which to cross safely would require great care.

But the gale was threatening, and the harbour inside, we could see, was smooth; then, too, cried my people: "Any port in a storm." I decided prompt; put the helm up and squared away. Flying thence, before it, the tempest-tossed canoe came sweeping in from sea over the rollers in a delightfully thrilling way. One breaker only coming over us, and even that did no harm more than to give us all the climax soaking of the voyage. This was the last sea that broke over the canoe on the memorable voyage.

The harbour inside the bar of New River was good. Adding much to our comfort too was fish and game in abundance.

The *Packet*, which had parted from us, made her destined port some three leagues farther on. The last we saw of the children, they were at the main sheets hauling aft, and their father was at the helm, and all were flying through the mist like fearless sailors.

After meeting Carolina seamen, to say nothing of the few still in existence further north, I challenge the story of Greek supremacy.

The little town of South Port was made up almost entirely of pilots possessing, I am sure, every quality of the sailor and the gentleman.

Moored snug in the inlet, it was pleasant to listen to the roar of the breakers on the bar, but not so cheerful was the thought of facing the high waves seaward. Therefore the plan suggested itself of sufficiently deepening a ditch that led through the marshes from New River to Bogue Sound, to let us through; thence we could sail inland the rest of the voyage without obstruction or hindrance of any kind. To this end we set about contrivances to heave the canoe over the shoals, and borrowed a shovel from a friendly schooner captain to deepen the ditch which we thought would be necessary to do in order to ford her along that way. However, the prevailing nor'east gales had so raised the water in the west end of the sound as to fill all the creeks and ditches to overflowing. I hesitated then no longer, but heading for the ditch through the marshes on a high tide, before a brave west wind took the chances of getting through by hook or by crook or by shovel and spade if required.

The "Coast Pilot," in speaking of this place, says there is never more than a foot of water there, and even that much is rarely found. The *Liberdade* essayed the ditch, drawing two feet and four inches, thus showing the further good fortune or luck which followed perseverance, as it usually does, though sometimes, maybe, it is bad luck! Perhaps I am not lucid on this, which at best must remain a disputed point.

I was getting lost in the maze of sloughs and creeks, which as soon as I entered seemed to lead in every direction but the right one. Hailing a hunter near by, however, I was soon put straight and reassured of success. The most astonished man, though, in North Carolina, was this same hunter when asked if he knew the ditch that led through where I wished to go.

"Why, stranger," said he, "my gran'ther digged that ditch."

I jumped, I leaped! at thought of what a pilot this man would be.

"Well, stranger," said he, in reply to my query, "stranger, if any man kin take y' thro' that ditch, why, I kin"; adding doubtfully, however, "I have not hearn tell befo' of a vessel from Brazil sailing through these parts; but then you mout get through, and again ye moutent. Well, it's jist here; you mout and you moutent."

A bargain was quickly made, and my pilot came aboard, armed with a long gun, which as we sailed along proved a terror to ducks. The entrance to the ditch, then close by, was made with a flowing sheet, and I soon found that my pilot knew his business. Rush-swamps and corn-fields we left to port and to starboard, and were at times out of sight among brakes that brushed crackling along the sides of the canoe, as she swept briskly through the narrows, passing them all, with many a close hug, though, on all sides. At a point well on in the crooked channel my pilot threw up his hat, and shouted, with all his might:

"Yer trouble is over! Swan to gosh if it ain't! And ye come all the way from Brazil, and come through gran'ther's ditch! Well, I d'clar!"

From this I concluded that we had cleared all the doubtful places, and so it turned out. Before sundown my pilot was looking for the change of a five-dollar-piece; and we of the *Liberdade* sat before a pot-pie, at twilight, the like of which on the whole voyage had not been tasted, from sea fowl laid about by our pilot while sailing through the meadows and marshes. And the pilot himself, returning while the pot-pie was yet steaming hot, declared it "ahead of coon."

A pleasant sail was this through the ditch that gran'ther dug. At the camp fire that night, where we hauled up by a fishing station, thirty stalwart men talked over the adventures of their lives. My pilot, the best speaker, kept the camp in roars. As for myself, always fond of mirth, I got up from the fire sore from laughing. Their curious adventures with coons and 'gators recounted had been considerable.

Many startling stories were told. But frequently reverting to the voyage of the *Liberdade*, they declared with one voice that "it was the greatest thing since the

114

wah." I took this as a kind of complimentary hospitality. "When she struck on a sand reef," said the pilot, "why, the captain he jumped right overboard and the son he jumped right over, too, to tote her over, and the captain's wife she holp."

By daylight next morning we sailed from this camp pleasant, and on the following day, November 28, at noon, arrived at Beaufort.

Mayor Bell of that city and many of his townfolk met us at the wharf, and gave me as well as my sea-tossed crew a welcome to their shores, such as to make us feel that the country was partly ours.

"Welcome, welcome home," said the good mayor; "we have read of your adventures, and watched your progress as reported from time to time, with deep interest and sympathy."

So we began to learn now that prayers on shore had gone up for the little canoe at sea. This was indeed America and home, for which we had longed while thousands of miles across the ocean.

From Beaufort to Norfolk and thence to Washington was pleasant inland sailing, with prevailing fair winds and smooth sea. Christmas was spent on the Chesa-peake—a fine, enjoyable day it was! with not a white-cap ripple on the bay. Ducks swimming ahead of the canoe as she moved quietly along were loath to take wing in so light a breeze, but flapping away, half paddling and half flying, as we came toward them, they managed to keep a long gun-shot off; but having laid in at the last port a turkey of no mean proportions, which we made shift to roast in the "caboose" aboard, we could look at a duck without wishing its destruction. With this turkey and a bountiful plum duff, we made out a dinner even on the *Liberdade*.

Of the many Christmas days that come crowding in

my recollections now; days spent on the sea and in foreign lands, as falls to the lot of sailors—which was the merriest it would be hard to say. Of this, however, I am certain, that the one on board the *Liberdade* on the Chesapeake was not the least happy of them all.

The day following Christmas found us on the Potomac, enjoying the same fine weather and abundant good cheer of the day before. Fair winds carried us through all the reaches of the river, and the same prosperity which attended our little bark in the beginning of the voyage through tempestuous weather followed her to the end of the voyage, which terminated in mild days and pleasant sunshine.

On the 27th of December, 1888, a south wind bore us into harbour at Washington, D.C., there we moored for the winter, furled our sails and coiled up the ropes, after a voyage of joys and sorrows, crowned with pleasures, however, which lessened the pain of past regrets.

Having moored the *Liberdade* and weather-bitted her cables, it remains only to be said that after bringing us safely through the dangers of a tropical voyage, clearing reefs, shoals, breakers, and all storms without a serious accident of any kind, we learned to love the little canoe as well as anything could be loved that is made by hands.

To say that we had not a moment of ill-health on the voyage would not tell the whole story.

My wife, brave enough to face the worst storms, as women are sometimes known to do on sea and on land, enjoyed not only the best of health, but had gained a richer complexion.

Victor, at the end of the voyage, found that he had grown an inch and had not been frightened out of his boots.

VOYAGE ENDED

Little Garfield—well he had grown some, too, and continued to be a pretty good boy and had managed to hold his grip through many ups and downs. He it was who stood by the bow line to make fast as quick as the *Liberdade* came to the pier at the end of the voyage.

And I, last, as it should be, lost a few pounds' weight, but like the rest landed in perfect health; taking it altogether, therefore, only pleasant recollections of the voyage remain with us who made it.

With all its vicissitudes I still love a life on the broad, free ocean, never regretting the choice of my profession.

However, the time has come to debark from the *Liberdade*, now breasted to the pier where I leave her for a time; for my people are landed safe in port.

DISPOSAL OF THE LIBERDADE

ABOUT the middle of April the *Liberdade* cast loose her moorings from the dock at Washington, and spreading sail before a brave west wind, bent her course along down the Potomac with the same facility as experienced in December coming up before a wind from the South; then shaping her course for New York via Baltimore and Philadelphia through inland passages, the voyage was turned into a pleasure excursion. Animation of spring clothed the landscape on all sides in its greatest beauty; and our northern forest the voyagers found upon their return was not less charming than "tropic shade" of foreign climes. And the robin sang even a sweeter trill than ever before heard by the crew, for they listened to it now in the country that they loved.

From New York, the *Liberdade* sailed for Boston via New London, New Bedford, Martha's Vineyard, Newport, and Taunton, at which latter place she hauled out, and the crew, thence to the Bay State Capital, enjoyed the novelty of a "sail over land."

Then the *Liberdade* moored snug in Boston and her crew spent the winter again among friends. They met here during this time the man who advised the captain at Buenos Aires to pitch the *Aquidneck's* cargo of hay into the sea; for not taking the advice—witness, alas! the captain's plight!

Finally, upon return of spring, the *Liberdade* was re-fitted on a voyage retracing her course to Washington, where, following safe arrival, she will end her days in the Smithsonian Institution; a haven of honour that many will be glad to know she has won.

A CATALOG OF SELECTED
DOVER BOOKS
IN ALL FIELDS OF INTEREST

A CATALOG OF SELECTED DOVER
BOOKS IN ALL FIELDS OF INTEREST

CONCERNING THE SPIRITUAL IN ART, Wassily Kandinsky. Pioneering work by father of abstract art. Thoughts on color theory, nature of art. Analysis of earlier masters. 12 illustrations. 80pp. of text. 5⅜ x 8½.   23411-8 Pa. $4.95

ANIMALS: 1,419 Copyright-Free Illustrations of Mammals, Birds, Fish, Insects, etc., Jim Harter (ed.). Clear wood engravings present, in extremely lifelike poses, over 1,000 species of animals. One of the most extensive pictorial sourcebooks of its kind. Captions. Index. 284pp. 9 x 12.   23766-4 Pa. $14.95

CELTIC ART: The Methods of Construction, George Bain. Simple geometric techniques for making Celtic interlacements, spirals, Kells-type initials, animals, humans, etc. Over 500 illustrations. 160pp. 9 x 12. (USO)   22923-8 Pa. $9.95

AN ATLAS OF ANATOMY FOR ARTISTS, Fritz Schider. Most thorough reference work on art anatomy in the world. Hundreds of illustrations, including selections from works by Vesalius, Leonardo, Goya, Ingres, Michelangelo, others. 593 illustrations. 192pp. 7⅞ x 10¼.   20241-0 Pa. $9.95

CELTIC HAND STROKE-BY-STROKE (Irish Half-Uncial from "The Book of Kells"): An Arthur Baker Calligraphy Manual, Arthur Baker. Complete guide to creating each letter of the alphabet in distinctive Celtic manner. Covers hand position, strokes, pens, inks, paper, more. Illustrated. 48pp. 8¼ x 11.   24336-2 Pa. $3.95

EASY ORIGAMI, John Montroll. Charming collection of 32 projects (hat, cup, pelican, piano, swan, many more) specially designed for the novice origami hobbyist. Clearly illustrated easy-to-follow instructions insure that even beginning papercrafters will achieve successful results. 48pp. 8¼ x 11.   27298-2 Pa. $3.50

THE COMPLETE BOOK OF BIRDHOUSE CONSTRUCTION FOR WOODWORKERS, Scott D. Campbell. Detailed instructions, illustrations, tables. Also data on bird habitat and instinct patterns. Bibliography. 3 tables. 63 illustrations in 15 figures. 48pp. 5¼ x 8½.   24407-5 Pa. $2.50

BLOOMINGDALE'S ILLUSTRATED 1886 CATALOG: Fashions, Dry Goods and Housewares, Bloomingdale Brothers. Famed merchants' extremely rare catalog depicting about 1,700 products: clothing, housewares, firearms, dry goods, jewelry, more. Invaluable for dating, identifying vintage items. Also, copyright-free graphics for artists, designers. Co-published with Henry Ford Museum & Greenfield Village. 160pp. 8¼ x 11.   25780-0 Pa. $10.95

HISTORIC COSTUME IN PICTURES, Braun & Schneider. Over 1,450 costumed figures in clearly detailed engravings—from dawn of civilization to end of 19th century. Captions. Many folk costumes. 256pp. 8⅜ x 11¾.   23150-X Pa. $12.95

CATALOG OF DOVER BOOKS

STICKLEY CRAFTSMAN FURNITURE CATALOGS, Gustav Stickley and L. & J. G. Stickley. Beautiful, functional furniture in two authentic catalogs from 1910. 594 illustrations, including 277 photos, show settles, rockers, armchairs, reclining chairs, bookcases, desks, tables. 183pp. 6½ x 9¼.   23838-5 Pa. $11.95

AMERICAN LOCOMOTIVES IN HISTORIC PHOTOGRAPHS: 1858 to 1949, Ron Ziel (ed.). A rare collection of 126 meticulously detailed official photographs, called "builder portraits," of American locomotives that majestically chronicle the rise of steam locomotive power in America. Introduction. Detailed captions. xi + 129pp. 9 x 12.   27393-8 Pa. $13.95

AMERICA'S LIGHTHOUSES: An Illustrated History, Francis Ross Holland, Jr. Delightfully written, profusely illustrated fact-filled survey of over 200 American lighthouses since 1716. History, anecdotes, technological advances, more. 240pp. 8 x 10¾.   25576-X Pa. $12.95

TOWARDS A NEW ARCHITECTURE, Le Corbusier. Pioneering manifesto by founder of "International School." Technical and aesthetic theories, views of industry, economics, relation of form to function, "mass-production split" and much more. Profusely illustrated. 320pp. 6⅛ x 9¼. (USO)   25023-7 Pa. $9.95

HOW THE OTHER HALF LIVES, Jacob Riis. Famous journalistic record, exposing poverty and degradation of New York slums around 1900, by major social reformer. 100 striking and influential photographs. 233pp. 10 x 7⅞.   22012-5 Pa. $11.95

FRUIT KEY AND TWIG KEY TO TREES AND SHRUBS, William M. Harlow. One of the handiest and most widely used identification aids. Fruit key covers 120 deciduous and evergreen species; twig key 160 deciduous species. Easily used. Over 300 photographs. 126pp. 5⅜ x 8½.   20511-8 Pa. $3.95

COMMON BIRD SONGS, Dr. Donald J. Borror. Songs of 60 most common U.S. birds: robins, sparrows, cardinals, bluejays, finches, more—arranged in order of increasing complexity. Up to 9 variations of songs of each species.
Cassette and manual 99911-4 $8.95

ORCHIDS AS HOUSE PLANTS, Rebecca Tyson Northen. Grow cattleyas and many other kinds of orchids—in a window, in a case, or under artificial light. 63 illustrations. 148pp. 5⅜ x 8½.   23261-1 Pa. $5.95

MONSTER MAZES, Dave Phillips. Masterful mazes at four levels of difficulty. Avoid deadly perils and evil creatures to find magical treasures. Solutions for all 32 exciting illustrated puzzles. 48pp. 8¼ x 11.   26005-4 Pa. $2.95

MOZART'S DON GIOVANNI (DOVER OPERA LIBRETTO SERIES), Wolfgang Amadeus Mozart. Introduced and translated by Ellen H. Bleiler. Standard Italian libretto, with complete English translation. Convenient and thoroughly portable—an ideal companion for reading along with a recording or the performance itself. Introduction. List of characters. Plot summary. 121pp. 5¼ x 8½.   24944-1 Pa. $3.95

TECHNICAL MANUAL AND DICTIONARY OF CLASSICAL BALLET, Gail Grant. Defines, explains, comments on steps, movements, poses and concepts. 15-page pictorial section. Basic book for student, viewer. 127pp. 5⅜ x 8½.   21843-0 Pa. $4.95

THE CLARINET AND CLARINET PLAYING, David Pino. Lively, comprehensive work features suggestions about technique, musicianship, and musical interpretation, as well as guidelines for teaching, making your own reeds, and preparing for public performance. Includes an intriguing look at clarinet history. "A godsend," The Clarinet, Journal of the International Clarinet Society. Appendixes. 7 illus. 320pp. 5⅜ x 8½. 40270-3 Pa. $9.95

HOLLYWOOD GLAMOR PORTRAITS, John Kobal (ed.). 145 photos from 1926-49. Harlow, Gable, Bogart, Bacall; 94 stars in all. Full background on photographers, technical aspects. 160pp. 8⅜ x 11¼. 23352-9 Pa. $12.95

THE ANNOTATED CASEY AT THE BAT: A Collection of Ballads about the Mighty Casey/Third, Revised Edition, Martin Gardner (ed.). Amusing sequels and parodies of one of America's best-loved poems: Casey's Revenge, Why Casey Whiffed, Casey's Sister at the Bat, others. 256pp. 5⅜ x 8½. 28598-7 Pa. $8.95

THE RAVEN AND OTHER FAVORITE POEMS, Edgar Allan Poe. Over 40 of the author's most memorable poems: "The Bells," "Ulalume," "Israfel," "To Helen," "The Conqueror Worm," "Eldorado," "Annabel Lee," many more. Alphabetic lists of titles and first lines. 64pp. 5 3/16 x 8¼. 26685-0 Pa. $1.00

PERSONAL MEMOIRS OF U. S. GRANT, Ulysses Simpson Grant. Intelligent, deeply moving firsthand account of Civil War campaigns, considered by many the finest military memoirs ever written. Includes letters, historic photographs, maps and more. 528pp. 6⅛ x 9¼. 28587-1 Pa. $12.95

ANCIENT EGYPTIAN MATERIALS AND INDUSTRIES, A. Lucas and J. Harris. Fascinating, comprehensive, thoroughly documented text describes this ancient civilization's vast resources and the processes that incorporated them in daily life, including the use of animal products, building materials, cosmetics, perfumes and incense, fibers, glazed ware, glass and its manufacture, materials used in the mummification process, and much more. 544pp. 6⅛ x 9¼. (USO) 40446-3 Pa. $16.95

RUSSIAN STORIES/PYCCKNE PACCKA3bl: A Dual-Language Book, edited by Gleb Struve. Twelve tales by such masters as Chekhov, Tolstoy, Dostoevsky, Pushkin, others. Excellent word-for-word English translations on facing pages, plus teaching and study aids, Russian/English vocabulary, biographical/critical introductions, more. 416pp. 5⅜ x 8½. 26244-8 Pa. $9.95

PHILADELPHIA THEN AND NOW: 60 Sites Photographed in the Past and Present, Kenneth Finkel and Susan Oyama. Rare photographs of City Hall, Logan Square, Independence Hall, Betsy Ross House, other landmarks juxtaposed with contemporary views. Captures changing face of historic city. Introduction. Captions. 128pp. 8¼ x 11. 25790-8 Pa. $9.95

AIA ARCHITECTURAL GUIDE TO NASSAU AND SUFFOLK COUNTIES, LONG ISLAND, The American Institute of Architects, Long Island Chapter, and the Society for the Preservation of Long Island Antiquities. Comprehensive, well-researched and generously illustrated volume brings to life over three centuries of Long Island's great architectural heritage. More than 240 photographs with authoritative, extensively detailed captions. 176pp. 8¼ x 11. 26946-9 Pa. $14.95

NORTH AMERICAN INDIAN LIFE: Customs and Traditions of 23 Tribes, Elsie Clews Parsons (ed.). 27 fictionalized essays by noted anthropologists examine religion, customs, government, additional facets of life among the Winnebago, Crow, Zuni, Eskimo, other tribes. 480pp. 6⅛ x 9¼. 27377-6 Pa. $10.95

FRANK LLOYD WRIGHT'S DANA HOUSE, Donald Hoffmann. Pictorial essay of residential masterpiece with over 160 interior and exterior photos, plans, elevations, sketches and studies. 128pp. 9¼ x 10¾.   29120-0 Pa. $12.95

THE MALE AND FEMALE FIGURE IN MOTION: 60 Classic Photographic Sequences, Eadweard Muybridge. 60 true-action photographs of men and women walking, running, climbing, bending, turning, etc., reproduced from rare 19th-century masterpiece. vi + 121pp. 9 x 12.   24745-7 Pa. $10.95

1001 QUESTIONS ANSWERED ABOUT THE SEASHORE, N. J. Berrill and Jacquelyn Berrill. Queries answered about dolphins, sea snails, sponges, starfish, fishes, shore birds, many others. Covers appearance, breeding, growth, feeding, much more. 305pp. 5¼ x 8¼.   23366-9 Pa. $9.95

ATTRACTING BIRDS TO YOUR YARD, William J. Weber. Easy-to-follow guide offers advice on how to attract the greatest diversity of birds: birdhouses, feeders, water and waterers, much more. 96pp. 5³⁄₁₆ x 8¼.   28927-3 Pa. $2.50

MEDICINAL AND OTHER USES OF NORTH AMERICAN PLANTS: A Historical Survey with Special Reference to the Eastern Indian Tribes, Charlotte Erichsen-Brown. Chronological historical citations document 500 years of usage of plants, trees, shrubs native to eastern Canada, northeastern U.S. Also complete identifying information. 343 illustrations. 544pp. 6½ x 9¼.   25951-X Pa. $12.95

STORYBOOK MAZES, Dave Phillips. 23 stories and mazes on two-page spreads: Wizard of Oz, Treasure Island, Robin Hood, etc. Solutions. 64pp. 8¼ x 11.
            23628-5 Pa. $2.95

AMERICAN NEGRO SONGS: 230 Folk Songs and Spirituals, Religious and Secular, John W. Work. This authoritative study traces the African influences of songs sung and played by black Americans at work, in church, and as entertainment. The author discusses the lyric significance of such songs as "Swing Low, Sweet Chariot," "John Henry," and others and offers the words and music for 230 songs. Bibliography. Index of Song Titles. 272pp. 6½ x 9¼.   40271-1 Pa. $9.95

MOVIE-STAR PORTRAITS OF THE FORTIES, John Kobal (ed.). 163 glamor, studio photos of 106 stars of the 1940s: Rita Hayworth, Ava Gardner, Marlon Brando, Clark Gable, many more. 176pp. 8⅜ x 11¼.   23546-7 Pa. $14.95

BENCHLEY LOST AND FOUND, Robert Benchley. Finest humor from early 30s, about pet peeves, child psychologists, post office and others. Mostly unavailable elsewhere. 73 illustrations by Peter Arno and others. 183pp. 5⅜ x 8½. 22410-4 Pa. $6.95

YEKL and THE IMPORTED BRIDEGROOM AND OTHER STORIES OF YIDDISH NEW YORK, Abraham Cahan. Film Hester Street based on Yekl (1896). Novel, other stories among first about Jewish immigrants on N.Y.'s East Side. 240pp. 5⅜ x 8½.   22427-9 Pa. $6.95

SELECTED POEMS, Walt Whitman. Generous sampling from *Leaves of Grass*. Twenty-four poems include "I Hear America Singing," "Song of the Open Road," "I Sing the Body Electric," "When Lilacs Last in the Dooryard Bloom'd," "O Captain! My Captain!"—all reprinted from an authoritative edition. Lists of titles and first lines. 128pp. 5³⁄₁₆ x 8¼.   26878-0 Pa. $1.00

CATALOG OF DOVER BOOKS

THE BEST TALES OF HOFFMANN, E. T. A. Hoffmann. 10 of Hoffmann's most important stories: "Nutcracker and the King of Mice," "The Golden Flowerpot," etc. 458pp. 5⅜ x 8½. 21793-0 Pa. $9.95

FROM FETISH TO GOD IN ANCIENT EGYPT, E. A. Wallis Budge. Rich detailed survey of Egyptian conception of "God" and gods, magic, cult of animals, Osiris, more. Also, superb English translations of hymns and legends. 240 illustrations. 545pp. 5⅜ x 8½. 25803-3 Pa. $13.95

FRENCH STORIES/CONTES FRANÇAIS: A Dual-Language Book, Wallace Fowlie. Ten stories by French masters, Voltaire to Camus: "Micromegas" by Voltaire; "The Atheist's Mass" by Balzac; "Minuet" by de Maupassant; "The Guest" by Camus, six more. Excellent English translations on facing pages. Also French-English vocabulary list, exercises, more. 352pp. 5⅜ x 8½. 26443-2 Pa. $9.95

CHICAGO AT THE TURN OF THE CENTURY IN PHOTOGRAPHS: 122 Historic Views from the Collections of the Chicago Historical Society, Larry A. Viskochil. Rare large-format prints offer detailed views of City Hall, State Street, the Loop, Hull House, Union Station, many other landmarks, circa 1904-1913. Introduction. Captions. Maps. 144pp. 9⅜ x 12¼. 24656-6 Pa. $12.95

OLD BROOKLYN IN EARLY PHOTOGRAPHS, 1865-1929, William Lee Younger. Luna Park, Gravesend race track, construction of Grand Army Plaza, moving of Hotel Brighton, etc. 157 previously unpublished photographs. 165pp. 8⅞ x 11¾. 23587-4 Pa. $13.95

THE MYTHS OF THE NORTH AMERICAN INDIANS, Lewis Spence. Rich anthology of the myths and legends of the Algonquins, Iroquois, Pawnees and Sioux, prefaced by an extensive historical and ethnological commentary. 36 illustrations. 480pp. 5⅜ x 8½. 25967-6 Pa. $10.95

AN ENCYCLOPEDIA OF BATTLES: Accounts of Over 1,560 Battles from 1479 B.C. to the Present, David Eggenberger. Essential details of every major battle in recorded history from the first battle of Megiddo in 1479 B.C. to Grenada in 1984. List of Battle Maps. New Appendix covering the years 1967-1984. Index. 99 illustrations. 544pp. 6½ x 9¼. 24913-1 Pa. $16.95

SAILING ALONE AROUND THE WORLD, Captain Joshua Slocum. First man to sail around the world, alone, in small boat. One of great feats of seamanship told in delightful manner. 67 illustrations. 294pp. 5⅜ x 8½. 20326-3 Pa. $6.95

ANARCHISM AND OTHER ESSAYS, Emma Goldman. Powerful, penetrating, prophetic essays on direct action, role of minorities, prison reform, puritan hypocrisy, violence, etc. 271pp. 5⅜ x 8½. 22484-8 Pa. $7.95

MYTHS OF THE HINDUS AND BUDDHISTS, Ananda K. Coomaraswamy and Sister Nivedita. Great stories of the epics; deeds of Krishna, Shiva, taken from puranas, Vedas, folk tales; etc. 32 illustrations. 400pp. 5⅜ x 8½. 21759-0 Pa. $12.95

THE TRAUMA OF BIRTH, Otto Rank. Rank's controversial thesis that anxiety neurosis is caused by profound psychological trauma which occurs at birth. 256pp. 5⅜ x 8½. 27974-X Pa. $7.95

A THEOLOGICO-POLITICAL TREATISE, Benedict Spinoza. Also contains unfinished Political Treatise. Great classic on religious liberty, theory of government on common consent. R. Elwes translation. Total of 421pp. 5⅜ x 8½. 20249-6 Pa. $9.95

CATALOG OF DOVER BOOKS

MY BONDAGE AND MY FREEDOM, Frederick Douglass. Born a slave, Douglass became outspoken force in antislavery movement. The best of Douglass' autobiographies. Graphic description of slave life. 464pp. 5⅜ x 8½. 22457-0 Pa. $8.95

FOLLOWING THE EQUATOR: A Journey Around the World, Mark Twain. Fascinating humorous account of 1897 voyage to Hawaii, Australia, India, New Zealand, etc. Ironic, bemused reports on peoples, customs, climate, flora and fauna, politics, much more. 197 illustrations. 720pp. 5⅜ x 8½. 26113-1 Pa. $15.95

THE PEOPLE CALLED SHAKERS, Edward D. Andrews. Definitive study of Shakers: origins, beliefs, practices, dances, social organization, furniture and crafts, etc. 33 illustrations. 351pp. 5⅜ x 8½. 21081-2 Pa. $8.95

THE MYTHS OF GREECE AND ROME, H. A. Guerber. A classic of mythology, generously illustrated, long prized for its simple, graphic, accurate retelling of the principal myths of Greece and Rome, and for its commentary on their origins and significance. With 64 illustrations by Michelangelo, Raphael, Titian, Rubens, Canova, Bernini and others. 480pp. 5⅜ x 8½. 27584-1 Pa. $9.95

PSYCHOLOGY OF MUSIC, Carl E. Seashore. Classic work discusses music as a medium from psychological viewpoint. Clear treatment of physical acoustics, auditory apparatus, sound perception, development of musical skills, nature of musical feeling, host of other topics. 88 figures. 408pp. 5⅜ x 8½. 21851-1 Pa. $11.95

THE PHILOSOPHY OF HISTORY, Georg W. Hegel. Great classic of Western thought develops concept that history is not chance but rational process, the evolution of freedom. 457pp. 5⅜ x 8½. 20112-0 Pa. $9.95

THE BOOK OF TEA, Kakuzo Okakura. Minor classic of the Orient: entertaining, charming explanation, interpretation of traditional Japanese culture in terms of tea ceremony. 94pp. 5⅜ x 8½. 20070-1 Pa. $3.95

LIFE IN ANCIENT EGYPT, Adolf Erman. Fullest, most thorough, detailed older account with much not in more recent books, domestic life, religion, magic, medicine, commerce, much more. Many illustrations reproduce tomb paintings, carvings, hieroglyphs, etc. 597pp. 5⅜ x 8½. 22632-8 Pa. $12.95

SUNDIALS, Their Theory and Construction, Albert Waugh. Far and away the best, most thorough coverage of ideas, mathematics concerned, types, construction, adjusting anywhere. Simple, nontechnical treatment allows even children to build several of these dials. Over 100 illustrations. 230pp. 5⅜ x 8½. 22947-5 Pa. $8.95

THEORETICAL HYDRODYNAMICS, L. M. Milne-Thomson. Classic exposition of the mathematical theory of fluid motion, applicable to both hydrodynamics and aerodynamics. Over 600 exercises. 768pp. 6⅛ x 9¼. 68970-0 Pa. $20.95

SONGS OF EXPERIENCE: Facsimile Reproduction with 26 Plates in Full Color, William Blake. 26 full-color plates from a rare 1826 edition. Includes "TheTyger," "London," "Holy Thursday," and other poems. Printed text of poems. 48pp. 5¼ x 7. 24636-1 Pa. $4.95

OLD-TIME VIGNETTES IN FULL COLOR, Carol Belanger Grafton (ed.). Over 390 charming, often sentimental illustrations, selected from archives of Victorian graphics—pretty women posing, children playing, food, flowers, kittens and puppies, smiling cherubs, birds and butterflies, much more. All copyright-free. 48pp. 9¼ x 12¼. 27269-9 Pa. $7.95

PERSPECTIVE FOR ARTISTS, Rex Vicat Cole. Depth, perspective of sky and sea, shadows, much more, not usually covered. 391 diagrams, 81 reproductions of drawings and paintings. 279pp. 5⅜ x 8½. 22487-2 Pa. $7.95

DRAWING THE LIVING FIGURE, Joseph Sheppard. Innovative approach to artistic anatomy focuses on specifics of surface anatomy, rather than muscles and bones. Over 170 drawings of live models in front, back and side views, and in widely varying poses. Accompanying diagrams. 177 illustrations. Introduction. Index. 144pp. 8⅜ x11¼. 26723-7 Pa. $8.95

GOTHIC AND OLD ENGLISH ALPHABETS: 100 Complete Fonts, Dan X. Solo. Add power, elegance to posters, signs, other graphics with 100 stunning copyright-free alphabets: Blackstone, Dolbey, Germania, 97 more–including many lower-case, numerals, punctuation marks. 104pp. 8⅛ x 11. 24695-7 Pa. $8.95

HOW TO DO BEADWORK, Mary White. Fundamental book on craft from simple projects to five-bead chains and woven works. 106 illustrations. 142pp. 5⅜ x 8. 20697-1 Pa. $5.95

THE BOOK OF WOOD CARVING, Charles Marshall Sayers. Finest book for beginners discusses fundamentals and offers 34 designs. "Absolutely first rate . . . well thought out and well executed."–E. J. Tangerman. 118pp. 7¾ x 10⅝. 23654-4 Pa. $7.95

ILLUSTRATED CATALOG OF CIVIL WAR MILITARY GOODS: Union Army Weapons, Insignia, Uniform Accessories, and Other Equipment, Schuyler, Hartley, and Graham. Rare, profusely illustrated 1846 catalog includes Union Army uniform and dress regulations, arms and ammunition, coats, insignia, flags, swords, rifles, etc. 226 illustrations. 160pp. 9 x 12. 24939-5 Pa. $10.95

WOMEN'S FASHIONS OF THE EARLY 1900s: An Unabridged Republication of "New York Fashions, 1909," National Cloak & Suit Co. Rare catalog of mail-order fashions documents women's and children's clothing styles shortly after the turn of the century. Captions offer full descriptions, prices. Invaluable resource for fashion, costume historians. Approximately 725 illustrations. 128pp. 8⅜ x 11¼. 27276-1 Pa. $11.95

THE 1912 AND 1915 GUSTAV STICKLEY FURNITURE CATALOGS, Gustav Stickley. With over 200 detailed illustrations and descriptions, these two catalogs are essential reading and reference materials and identification guides for Stickley furniture. Captions cite materials, dimensions and prices. 112pp. 6½ x 9¼. 26676-1 Pa. $9.95

EARLY AMERICAN LOCOMOTIVES, John H. White, Jr. Finest locomotive engravings from early 19th century: historical (1804–74), main-line (after 1870), special, foreign, etc. 147 plates. 142pp. 11⅜ x 8¼. 22772-3 Pa. $10.95

THE TALL SHIPS OF TODAY IN PHOTOGRAPHS, Frank O. Braynard. Lavishly illustrated tribute to nearly 100 majestic contemporary sailing vessels: Amerigo Vespucci, Clearwater, Constitution, Eagle, Mayflower, Sea Cloud, Victory, many more. Authoritative captions provide statistics, background on each ship. 190 black-and-white photographs and illustrations. Introduction. 128pp. 8⅞ x 11¾. 27163-3 Pa. $14.95

LITTLE BOOK OF EARLY AMERICAN CRAFTS AND TRADES, Peter Stockham (ed.). 1807 children's book explains crafts and trades: baker, hatter, cooper, potter, and many others. 23 copperplate illustrations. 140pp. 4⅝ x 6.
23336-7 Pa. $4.95

VICTORIAN FASHIONS AND COSTUMES FROM HARPER'S BAZAR, 1867–1898, Stella Blum (ed.). Day costumes, evening wear, sports clothes, shoes, hats, other accessories in over 1,000 detailed engravings. 320pp. 9⅜ x 12¼.
22990-4 Pa. $15.95

GUSTAV STICKLEY, THE CRAFTSMAN, Mary Ann Smith. Superb study surveys broad scope of Stickley's achievement, especially in architecture. Design philosophy, rise and fall of the Craftsman empire, descriptions and floor plans for many Craftsman houses, more. 86 black-and-white halftones. 31 line illustrations. Introduction 208pp. 6½ x 9¼. 27210-9 Pa. $9.95

THE LONG ISLAND RAIL ROAD IN EARLY PHOTOGRAPHS, Ron Ziel. Over 220 rare photos, informative text document origin (1844) and development of rail service on Long Island. Vintage views of early trains, locomotives, stations, passengers, crews, much more. Captions. 8⅞ x 11¾. 26301-0 Pa. $13.95

VOYAGE OF THE LIBERDADE, Joshua Slocum. Great 19th-century mariner's thrilling, first-hand account of the wreck of his ship off South America, the 35-foot boat he built from the wreckage, and its remarkable voyage home. 128pp. 5⅜ x 8½.
40022-0 Pa. $4.95

TEN BOOKS ON ARCHITECTURE, Vitruvius. The most important book ever written on architecture. Early Roman aesthetics, technology, classical orders, site selection, all other aspects. Morgan translation. 331pp. 5⅜ x 8½. 20645-9 Pa. $8.95

THE HUMAN FIGURE IN MOTION, Eadweard Muybridge. More than 4,500 stopped-action photos, in action series, showing undraped men, women, children jumping, lying down, throwing, sitting, wrestling, carrying, etc. 390pp. 7⅞ x 10⅝.
20204-6 Clothbd. $27.95

TREES OF THE EASTERN AND CENTRAL UNITED STATES AND CANADA, William M. Harlow. Best one-volume guide to 140 trees. Full descriptions, woodlore, range, etc. Over 600 illustrations. Handy size. 288pp. 4½ x 6⅜.
20395-6 Pa. $6.95

SONGS OF WESTERN BIRDS, Dr. Donald J. Borror. Complete song and call repertoire of 60 western species, including flycatchers, juncoes, cactus wrens, many more–includes fully illustrated booklet. Cassette and manual 99913-0 $8.95

GROWING AND USING HERBS AND SPICES, Milo Miloradovich. Versatile handbook provides all the information needed for cultivation and use of all the herbs and spices available in North America. 4 illustrations. Index. Glossary. 236pp. 5⅜ x 8½.
25058-X Pa. $7.95

BIG BOOK OF MAZES AND LABYRINTHS, Walter Shepherd. 50 mazes and labyrinths in all–classical, solid, ripple, and more–in one great volume. Perfect inexpensive puzzler for clever youngsters. Full solutions. 112pp. 8⅛ x 11.
22951-3 Pa. $5.95

PIANO TUNING, J. Cree Fischer. Clearest, best book for beginner, amateur. Simple repairs, raising dropped notes, tuning by easy method of flattened fifths. No previous skills needed. 4 illustrations. 201pp. 5⅜ x 8½. 23267-0 Pa. $6.95

HINTS TO SINGERS, Lillian Nordica. Selecting the right teacher, developing confidence, overcoming stage fright, and many other important skills receive thoughtful discussion in this indispensible guide, written by a world-famous diva of four decades' experience. 96pp. 5³/₈ x 8¹/₂. 40094-8 Pa. $4.95

THE COMPLETE NONSENSE OF EDWARD LEAR, Edward Lear. All nonsense limericks, zany alphabets, Owl and Pussycat, songs, nonsense botany, etc., illustrated by Lear. Total of 320pp. 5⅜ x 8½. (USO) 20167-8 Pa. $7.95

VICTORIAN PARLOUR POETRY: An Annotated Anthology, Michael R. Turner. 117 gems by Longfellow, Tennyson, Browning, many lesser-known poets. "The Village Blacksmith," "Curfew Must Not Ring Tonight," "Only a Baby Small," dozens more, often difficult to find elsewhere. Index of poets, titles, first lines. xxiii + 325pp. 5⅜ x 8¼. 27044-0 Pa. $8.95

DUBLINERS, James Joyce. Fifteen stories offer vivid, tightly focused observations of the lives of Dublin's poorer classes. At least one, "The Dead," is considered a masterpiece. Reprinted complete and unabridged from standard edition. 160pp. 5⅜₆ x 8¼. 26870-5 Pa. $1.00

GREAT WEIRD TALES: 14 Stories by Lovecraft, Blackwood, Machen and Others, S. T. Joshi (ed.). 14 spellbinding tales, including "The Sin Eater," by Fiona McLeod, "The Eye Above the Mantel," by Frank Belknap Long, as well as renowned works by R. H. Barlow, Lord Dunsany, Arthur Machen, W. C. Morrow and eight other masters of the genre. 256pp. 5⅜ x 8½. (USO) 40436-6 Pa. $8.95

THE BOOK OF THE SACRED MAGIC OF ABRAMELIN THE MAGE, translated by S. MacGregor Mathers. Medieval manuscript of ceremonial magic. Basic document in Aleister Crowley, Golden Dawn groups. 268pp. 5⅜ x 8½. 23211-5 Pa. $9.95

NEW RUSSIAN-ENGLISH AND ENGLISH-RUSSIAN DICTIONARY, M. A. O'Brien. This is a remarkably handy Russian dictionary, containing a surprising amount of information, including over 70,000 entries. 366pp. 4½ x 6⅛. 20208-9 Pa. $10.95

HISTORIC HOMES OF THE AMERICAN PRESIDENTS, Second, Revised Edition, Irvin Haas. A traveler's guide to American Presidential homes, most open to the public, depicting and describing homes occupied by every American President from George Washington to George Bush. With visiting hours, admission charges, travel routes. 175 photographs. Index. 160pp. 8¼ x 11. 26751-2 Pa. $11.95

NEW YORK IN THE FORTIES, Andreas Feininger. 162 brilliant photographs by the well-known photographer, formerly with *Life* magazine. Commuters, shoppers, Times Square at night, much else from city at its peak. Captions by John von Hartz. 181pp. 9¼ x 10¾. 23585-8 Pa. $13.95

INDIAN SIGN LANGUAGE, William Tomkins. Over 525 signs developed by Sioux and other tribes. Written instructions and diagrams. Also 290 pictographs. 111pp. 6⅛ x 9¼. 22029-X Pa. $3.95

ANATOMY: A Complete Guide for Artists, Joseph Sheppard. A master of figure drawing shows artists how to render human anatomy convincingly. Over 460 illustrations. 224pp. 8⅜ x 11¼. 27279-6 Pa. $11.95

MEDIEVAL CALLIGRAPHY: Its History and Technique, Marc Drogin. Spirited history, comprehensive instruction manual covers 13 styles (ca. 4th century thru 15th). Excellent photographs; directions for duplicating medieval techniques with modern tools. 224pp. 8⅜ x 11¼. 26142-5 Pa. $12.95

DRIED FLOWERS: How to Prepare Them, Sarah Whitlock and Martha Rankin. Complete instructions on how to use silica gel, meal and borax, perlite aggregate, sand and borax, glycerine and water to create attractive permanent flower arrangements. 12 illustrations. 32pp. 5⅜ x 8½. 21802-3 Pa. $1.00

EASY-TO-MAKE BIRD FEEDERS FOR WOODWORKERS, Scott D. Campbell. Detailed, simple-to-use guide for designing, constructing, caring for and using feeders. Text, illustrations for 12 classic and contemporary designs. 96pp. 5⅜ x 8½. 25847-5 Pa. $3.95

SCOTTISH WONDER TALES FROM MYTH AND LEGEND, Donald A. Mackenzie. 16 lively tales tell of giants rumbling down mountainsides, of a magic wand that turns stone pillars into warriors, of gods and goddesses, evil hags, powerful forces and more. 240pp. 5⅜ x 8½. 29677-6 Pa. $6.95

THE HISTORY OF UNDERCLOTHES, C. Willett Cunnington and Phyllis Cunnington. Fascinating, well-documented survey covering six centuries of English undergarments, enhanced with over 100 illustrations: 12th-century laced-up bodice, footed long drawers (1795), 19th-century bustles, 19th-century corsets for men, Victorian "bust improvers," much more. 272pp. 5⅜ x 8¼. 27124-2 Pa. $9.95

ARTS AND CRAFTS FURNITURE: The Complete Brooks Catalog of 1912, Brooks Manufacturing Co. Photos and detailed descriptions of more than 150 now very collectible furniture designs from the Arts and Crafts movement depict davenports, settees, buffets, desks, tables, chairs, bedsteads, dressers and more, all built of solid, quarter-sawed oak. Invaluable for students and enthusiasts of antiques, Americana and the decorative arts. 80pp. 6½ x 9¼. 27471-3 Pa. $8.95

WILBUR AND ORVILLE: A Biography of the Wright Brothers, Fred Howard. Definitive, crisply written study tells the full story of the brothers' lives and work. A vividly written biography, unparalleled in scope and color, that also captures the spirit of an extraordinary era. 560pp. 6⅛ x 9¼. 40297-5 Pa. $17.95

THE ARTS OF THE SAILOR: Knotting, Splicing and Ropework, Hervey Garrett Smith. Indispensable shipboard reference covers tools, basic knots and useful hitches; handsewing and canvas work, more. Over 100 illustrations. Delightful reading for sea lovers. 256pp. 5⅜ x 8½. 26440-8 Pa. $8.95

FRANK LLOYD WRIGHT'S FALLINGWATER: The House and Its History, Second, Revised Edition, Donald Hoffmann. A total revision—both in text and illustrations—of the standard document on Fallingwater, the boldest, most personal architectural statement of Wright's mature years, updated with valuable new material from the recently opened Frank Lloyd Wright Archives. "Fascinating"—*The New York Times*. 116 illustrations. 128pp. 9¼ x 10¾. 27430-6 Pa. $12.95

CATALOG OF DOVER BOOKS

PHOTOGRAPHIC SKETCHBOOK OF THE CIVIL WAR, Alexander Gardner. 100 photos taken on field during the Civil War. Famous shots of Manassas Harper's Ferry, Lincoln, Richmond, slave pens, etc. 244pp. 10⅝ x 8¼.   22731-6 Pa. $10.95

FIVE ACRES AND INDEPENDENCE, Maurice G. Kains. Great back-to-the-land classic explains basics of self-sufficient farming. The one book to get. 95 illustrations. 397pp. 5⅜ x 8½.   20974-1 Pa. $7.95

SONGS OF EASTERN BIRDS, Dr. Donald J. Borror. Songs and calls of 60 species most common to eastern U.S.: warblers, woodpeckers, flycatchers, thrushes, larks, many more in high-quality recording.   Cassette and manual 99912-2 $9.95

A MODERN HERBAL, Margaret Grieve. Much the fullest, most exact, most useful compilation of herbal material. Gigantic alphabetical encyclopedia, from aconite to zedoary, gives botanical information, medical properties, folklore, economic uses, much else. Indispensable to serious reader. 161 illustrations. 888pp. 6½ x 9¼. 2-vol. set. (USO)   Vol. I: 22798-7 Pa. $9.95
                                                              Vol. II: 22799-5 Pa. $9.95

HIDDEN TREASURE MAZE BOOK, Dave Phillips. Solve 34 challenging mazes accompanied by heroic tales of adventure. Evil dragons, people-eating plants, blood-thirsty giants, many more dangerous adversaries lurk at every twist and turn. 34 mazes, stories, solutions. 48pp. 8¼ x 11.   24566-7 Pa. $2.95

LETTERS OF W. A. MOZART, Wolfgang A. Mozart. Remarkable letters show bawdy wit, humor, imagination, musical insights, contemporary musical world; includes some letters from Leopold Mozart. 276pp. 5⅜ x 8½.   22859-2 Pa. $7.95

BASIC PRINCIPLES OF CLASSICAL BALLET, Agrippina Vaganova. Great Russian theoretician, teacher explains methods for teaching classical ballet. 118 illustrations. 175pp. 5⅜ x 8½.   22036-2 Pa. $5.95

THE JUMPING FROG, Mark Twain. Revenge edition. The original story of The Celebrated Jumping Frog of Calaveras County, a hapless French translation, and Twain's hilarious "retranslation" from the French. 12 illustrations. 66pp. 5⅜ x 8½.   22686-7 Pa. $3.95

BEST REMEMBERED POEMS, Martin Gardner (ed.). The 126 poems in this superb collection of 19th- and 20th-century British and American verse range from Shelley's "To a Skylark" to the impassioned "Renascence" of Edna St. Vincent Millay and to Edward Lear's whimsical "The Owl and the Pussycat." 224pp. 5⅜ x 8½.   27165-X Pa. $5.95

COMPLETE SONNETS, William Shakespeare. Over 150 exquisite poems deal with love, friendship, the tyranny of time, beauty's evanescence, death and other themes in language of remarkable power, precision and beauty. Glossary of archaic terms. 80pp. 5³⁄₁₆ x 8¼.   26686-9 Pa. $1.00

BODIES IN A BOOKSHOP, R. T. Campbell. Challenging mystery of blackmail and murder with ingenious plot and superbly drawn characters. In the best tradition of British suspense fiction. 192pp. 5⅜ x 8½.   24720-1 Pa. $6.95

THE WIT AND HUMOR OF OSCAR WILDE, Alvin Redman (ed.). More than 1,000 ripostes, paradoxes, wisecracks: Work is the curse of the drinking classes; I can resist everything except temptation; etc. 258pp. 5⅜ x 8½. 20602-5 Pa. $6.95

SHAKESPEARE LEXICON AND QUOTATION DICTIONARY, Alexander Schmidt. Full definitions, locations, shades of meaning in every word in plays and poems. More than 50,000 exact quotations. 1,485pp. 6½ x 9¼. 2-vol. set.
Vol. 1: 22726-X Pa. $17.95
Vol. 2: 22727-8 Pa. $17.95

SELECTED POEMS, Emily Dickinson. Over 100 best-known, best-loved poems by one of America's foremost poets, reprinted from authoritative early editions. No comparable edition at this price. Index of first lines. 64pp. 5³⁄₁₆ x 8¼. 26466-1 Pa. $1.00

THE INSIDIOUS DR. FU-MANCHU, Sax Rohmer. The first of the popular mystery series introduces a pair of English detectives to their archnemesis, the diabolical Dr. Fu-Manchu. Flavorful atmosphere, fast-paced action, and colorful characters enliven this classic of the genre. 208pp. 5³⁄₁₆ x 8¼. 29898-1 Pa. $2.00

THE MALLEUS MALEFICARUM OF KRAMER AND SPRENGER, translated by Montague Summers. Full text of most important witchhunter's "bible," used by both Catholics and Protestants. 278pp. 6⅝ x 10. 22802-9 Pa. $12.95

SPANISH STORIES/CUENTOS ESPAÑOLES: A Dual-Language Book, Angel Flores (ed.). Unique format offers 13 great stories in Spanish by Cervantes, Borges, others. Faithful English translations on facing pages. 352pp. 5⅜ x 8½. 25399-6 Pa. $8.95

GARDEN CITY, LONG ISLAND, IN EARLY PHOTOGRAPHS, 1869–1919, Mildred H. Smith. Handsome treasury of 118 vintage pictures, accompanied by carefully researched captions, document the Garden City Hotel fire (1899), the Vanderbilt Cup Race (1908), the first airmail flight departing from the Nassau Boulevard Aerodrome (1911), and much more. 96pp. 8⅞ x 11¾. 40669-5 Pa. $12.95

OLD QUEENS, N.Y., IN EARLY PHOTOGRAPHS, Vincent F. Seyfried and William Asadorian. Over 160 rare photographs of Maspeth, Jamaica, Jackson Heights, and other areas. Vintage views of DeWitt Clinton mansion, 1939 World's Fair and more. Captions. 192pp. 8⅞ x 11. 26358-4 Pa. $12.95

CAPTURED BY THE INDIANS: 15 Firsthand Accounts, 1750-1870, Frederick Drimmer. Astounding true historical accounts of grisly torture, bloody conflicts, relentless pursuits, miraculous escapes and more, by people who lived to tell the tale. 384pp. 5⅜ x 8½. 24901-8 Pa. $8.95

THE WORLD'S GREAT SPEECHES (Fourth Enlarged Edition), Lewis Copeland, Lawrence W. Lamm, and Stephen J. McKenna. Nearly 300 speeches provide public speakers with a wealth of updated quotes and inspiration–from Pericles' funeral oration and William Jennings Bryan's "Cross of Gold Speech" to Malcolm X's powerful words on the Black Revolution and Earl of Spenser's tribute to his sister, Diana, Princess of Wales. 944pp. 5⅜ x 8⅜. 40903-1 Pa. $15.95

THE BOOK OF THE SWORD, Sir Richard F. Burton. Great Victorian scholar/adventurer's eloquent, erudite history of the "queen of weapons"–from prehistory to early Roman Empire. Evolution and development of early swords, variations (sabre, broadsword, cutlass, scimitar, etc.), much more. 336pp. 6⅛ x 9¼. 25434-8 Pa. $9.95

AUTOBIOGRAPHY: The Story of My Experiments with Truth, Mohandas K. Gandhi. Boyhood, legal studies, purification, the growth of the Satyagraha (nonviolent protest) movement. Critical, inspiring work of the man responsible for the freedom of India. 480pp. 5⅜ x 8½. (USO) 24593-4 Pa. $8.95

CELTIC MYTHS AND LEGENDS, T. W. Rolleston. Masterful retelling of Irish and Welsh stories and tales. Cuchulain, King Arthur, Deirdre, the Grail, many more. First paperback edition. 58 full-page illustrations. 512pp. 5⅜ x 8½. 26507-2 Pa. $9.95

THE PRINCIPLES OF PSYCHOLOGY, William James. Famous long course complete, unabridged. Stream of thought, time perception, memory, experimental methods; great work decades ahead of its time. 94 figures. 1,391pp. 5⅜ x 8½. 2-vol. set.
Vol. I: 20381-6 Pa. $13.95
Vol. II: 20382-4 Pa. $14.95

THE WORLD AS WILL AND REPRESENTATION, Arthur Schopenhauer. Definitive English translation of Schopenhauer's life work, correcting more than 1,000 errors, omissions in earlier translations. Translated by E. F. J. Payne. Total of 1,269pp. 5⅜ x 8½. 2-vol. set. Vol. 1: 21761-2 Pa. $12.95
Vol. 2: 21762-0 Pa. $12.95

MAGIC AND MYSTERY IN TIBET, Madame Alexandra David-Neel. Experiences among lamas, magicians, sages, sorcerers, Bonpa wizards. A true psychic discovery. 32 illustrations. 321pp. 5⅜ x 8½. (USO) 22682-4 Pa. $9.95

THE EGYPTIAN BOOK OF THE DEAD, E. A. Wallis Budge. Complete reproduction of Ani's papyrus, finest ever found. Full hieroglyphic text, interlinear transliteration, word-for-word translation, smooth translation. 533pp. 6½ x 9¼.
21866-X Pa. $11.95

MATHEMATICS FOR THE NONMATHEMATICIAN, Morris Kline. Detailed, college-level treatment of mathematics in cultural and historical context, with numerous exercises. Recommended Reading Lists. Tables. Numerous figures. 641pp. 5⅜ x 8½.
24823-2 Pa. $11.95

PROBABILISTIC METHODS IN THE THEORY OF STRUCTURES, Isaac Elishakoff. Well-written introduction covers the elements of the theory of probability from two or more random variables, the reliability of such multivariable structures, the theory of random function, Monte Carlo methods of treating problems incapable of exact solution, and more. Examples. 502pp. 5³/₈ x 8¹/₂. 40691-1 Pa. $16.95

THE RIME OF THE ANCIENT MARINER, Gustave Doré, S. T. Coleridge. Doré's finest work; 34 plates capture moods, subtleties of poem. Flawless full-size reproductions printed on facing pages with authoritative text of poem. "Beautiful. Simply beautiful."–*Publisher's Weekly*. 77pp. 9¼ x 12. 22305-1 Pa. $7.95

NORTH AMERICAN INDIAN DESIGNS FOR ARTISTS AND CRAFTSPEOPLE, Eva Wilson. Over 360 authentic copyright-free designs adapted from Navajo blankets, Hopi pottery, Sioux buffalo hides, more. Geometrics, symbolic figures, plant and animal motifs, etc. 128pp. 8⅜ x 11. (EUK) 25341-4 Pa. $8.95

SCULPTURE: Principles and Practice, Louis Slobodkin. Step-by-step approach to clay, plaster, metals, stone; classical and modern. 253 drawings, photos. 255pp. 8⅛ x 11.
22960-2 Pa. $11.95

CATALOG OF DOVER BOOKS

THE INFLUENCE OF SEA POWER UPON HISTORY, 1660–1783, A. T. Mahan. Influential classic of naval history and tactics still used as text in war colleges. First paperback edition. 4 maps. 24 battle plans. 640pp. 5⅜ x 8½. 25509-3 Pa. $14.95

THE STORY OF THE TITANIC AS TOLD BY ITS SURVIVORS, Jack Winocour (ed.). What it was really like. Panic, despair, shocking inefficiency, and a little heroism. More thrilling than any fictional account. 26 illustrations. 320pp. 5⅜ x 8½. 20610-6 Pa. $8.95

FAIRY AND FOLK TALES OF THE IRISH PEASANTRY, William Butler Yeats (ed.). Treasury of 64 tales from the twilight world of Celtic myth and legend: "The Soul Cages," "The Kildare Pooka," "King O'Toole and his Goose," many more. Introduction and Notes by W. B. Yeats. 352pp. 5⅜ x 8½. 26941-8 Pa. $8.95

BUDDHIST MAHAYANA TEXTS, E. B. Cowell and Others (eds.). Superb, accurate translations of basic documents in Mahayana Buddhism, highly important in history of religions. The Buddha-karita of Asvaghosha, Larger Sukhavativyuha, more. 448pp. 5⅜ x 8½. 25552-2 Pa. $12.95

ONE TWO THREE . . . INFINITY: Facts and Speculations of Science, George Gamow. Great physicist's fascinating, readable overview of contemporary science: number theory, relativity, fourth dimension, entropy, genes, atomic structure, much more. 128 illustrations. Index. 352pp. 5⅜ x 8½. 25664-2 Pa. $8.95

EXPERIMENTATION AND MEASUREMENT, W. J. Youden. Introductory manual explains laws of measurement in simple terms and offers tips for achieving accuracy and minimizing errors. Mathematics of measurement, use of instruments, experimenting with machines. 1994 edition. Foreword. Preface. Introduction. Epilogue. Selected Readings. Glossary. Index. Tables and figures. 128pp. 5⅜ x 8½. 40451-X Pa. $6.95

DALÍ ON MODERN ART: The Cuckolds of Antiquated Modern Art, Salvador Dalí. Influential painter skewers modern art and its practitioners. Outrageous evaluations of Picasso, Cézanne, Turner, more. 15 renderings of paintings discussed. 44 calligraphic decorations by Dalí. 96pp. 5⅜ x 8½. (USO) 29220-7 Pa. $5.95

ANTIQUE PLAYING CARDS: A Pictorial History, Henry René D'Allemagne. Over 900 elaborate, decorative images from rare playing cards (14th–20th centuries): Bacchus, death, dancing dogs, hunting scenes, royal coats of arms, players cheating, much more. 96pp. 9¼ x 12¼. 29265-7 Pa. $12.95

MAKING FURNITURE MASTERPIECES: 30 Projects with Measured Drawings, Franklin H. Gottshall. Step-by-step instructions, illustrations for constructing handsome, useful pieces, among them a Sheraton desk, Chippendale chair, Spanish desk, Queen Anne table and a William and Mary dressing mirror. 224pp. 8⅛ x 11¼. 29338-6 Pa. $13.95

THE FOSSIL BOOK: A Record of Prehistoric Life, Patricia V. Rich et al. Profusely illustrated definitive guide covers everything from single-celled organisms and dinosaurs to birds and mammals and the interplay between climate and man. Over 1,500 illustrations. 760pp. 7½ x 10⅛. 29371-8 Pa. $29.95

Prices subject to change without notice.

Available at your book dealer or write for free catalog to Dept. GI, Dover Publications, Inc., 31 East 2nd St., Mineola, N.Y. 11501. Dover publishes more than 500 books each year on science, elementary and advanced mathematics, biology, music, art, literary history, social sciences and other areas.